Mental Toughness: Getting the Edge

Baseball Edition

Dr. Curt Ickes

MENTAL TOUGHNESS: GETTING THE EDGE
BASEBALL EDITION

ISBN: 978-0-615-34430-0
Published by IRC Holdings Ltd. Ashland, Ohio
Cover photo by: Steven McSweeny
Cover design by: Josh L. Hines
Internal Layout: Sarah Wells

Available Soon –
Mental Toughness: Getting the Edge
Softball Edition
For further information contact Dr. Curt Ickes at
cickes@ashland.edu

Table of Contents

Part I: Building a Mentally Tough Personality

Part II: Mental Toughness in Action

Acknowledgements

There are many people I would like to thank for helping to make this book a reality. First, I want to thank all of the players that I have worked with in the past. Your enthusiasm and feedback have been invaluable. Watching you succeed, as individuals and as entire teams, makes it all worthwhile.

I would also like to express my gratitude to the following baseball coaches: Drew Patton, Cody Castle, Justin Randall, Bryan Thrasher, Mike Wolf, Marc Wilkins, Dan Mager, and Tim Pettorini. I continue to learn from all of you and appreciate how well you communicate the value of the mental game to your players.

I want to especially thank two coaches: Coach John Schaly, Head Baseball Coach at Ashland University and Coach John Massarelli, Manager of the Lake Erie Crushers. Coach Schaly gave me my first opportunity to work with a college baseball program and continues to be extremely supportive of my work. I appreciate your baseball knowledge, passion for the game, and continued willingness to discuss the nuances of the mental game. I also want to thank Coach Massarelli for the chance to work with his professional team this past season. It was a great experience. John, I am appreciative of your welcoming spirit and strong belief in the mental game. Thanks to both of you.

I also want to thank my family for their support, patience, and understanding regarding the amount of time I dedicated to this project. I appreciate all of you very much.

Finally, this project would have never come to pass had it not been for my editor, Jen Kindbom. It has been 30 years since I sat in a college grammar course and it showed. I will be forever grateful for your encouragement, patience, and the much needed direction. Thank you, thank you, and thank you!

Part I

Building a Mentally Tough Personality

*"People ask me what I do in the winter when there's no baseball.
I'll tell you what I do. I stare out the window and wait for spring."*
~ *Rogers Hornsby*

Chapter 1

The Mental Game

"Poets are like baseball pitchers. Both have their moments. The intervals are the tough things." ~ Robert Frost

I watch a lot of baseball... a lot of baseball. It occurred to me one day that I watch it differently than I used to. I used to watch with an interest in strategy, scores, and outcomes. Now, I find myself paying very close attention to the behavior of the players. I am watching and asking: *What is he thinking? What is he feeling? What is he doing?*

These days when I watch baseball, I ask questions like...

1. Is he focusing on the process of getting ready for this pitch instead of thinking about the last one?
2. Is he *truly* and *completely* expecting success?
3. Did he take his breath? Is he relaxed?
4. Does he feel in control of the situation?
5. Right now, does he completely trust his ability?
6. Does he understand how to let go of what he can't control?
7. Is he having fun?
8. Did he use a focal point? Is his mind clear?
9. Does he have 100% external narrow focus?
10. Has he practiced with intention?
11. Did he visualize success?

12. Is he feeling a sense of personal power?
13. Has he been able to cope with past failures instead of allowing them to weigh on his mind?
14. Is he feeling confident about this next pitch?
15. Has he learned to treat himself like he treats his best friend?
16. Is he playing as a gamer instead of feeling like a victim of circumstance?
17. Does he have a release ready in case things do not go well?
18. Does he understand that if he has done it before, he can do it again?
19. Has he been working on his mental game?
20. Is he ready to win this battle – right now?

Critically think about your mental game. How would you answer these questions?

Our shared goal, beginning today, is to help you develop the skills necessary to answer "Yes" to each of these questions. With well-practiced and automatic mental toughness skills, you will:

- Have the **best chance** of *success on the very next pitch.*
- Have the **best chance** of *playing up to your physical potential.*
- Have the **best chance** of *playing more consistently.*
- Have the **best chance** of *helping your team win.*
- Have the **best chance** of *enjoying the game of baseball.*

It has been said many times: Baseball is a mental game. Most players and coaches understand that a great mental game is vital to success. The mental game becomes even more important as players advance in level of play because the physical talent begins to equalize. As players progress from youth league to high school to college and to the professional level, fewer and fewer are able to simply physically dominate opponents. When the physical talent is even, the edge goes to the player with the best mental approach.

The problem is few players and teams spend much time working on the mental game. Teams spend extra time on hitting, pitching, and fielding. In an effort to gain any edge, players will buy brand new bats, batting gloves, and all sorts of the latest training devices. While coaches and players see the importance of the mental game, they largely ignore it—a choice that doesn't make sense. It would be like a coach saying, "Yes, learning to field a ground ball is important in baseball, but we really don't work on it. Hitting? Yes, developing hitting skills would help, but I am not sure we have time for that."

So, why do so many players and teams ignore the mental game? While there are many possible reasons, my contention is that they simply do not know **how** to work on developing a great mental game. Well-meaning coaches, teammates, and fans will often yell to a struggling player "Relax, Be Confident, Focus." They know the goal, but few know **how** to get there. As a clinical psychologist, it would be like me telling a client after the first session, "Well, Mr. Smith, you are depressed. What you simply need to do is be happy." This advice is not very helpful!

Some players hope they will somehow *get* a great mental game. Somehow, if they play baseball long enough, they believe mental toughness will suddenly come to them. Unfortunately, most players aren't able to pick up all of the required mental skills on their own. They might get bits and pieces by chance, but most players do not get the whole package. Because of this assumption that mental toughness will magically happen, they do not make a conscious, intentional effort to work at it.

Other players erroneously believe they already have a solid mental game when, in fact, they do not. When all is going well, baseball is easy and fun. But as soon as things get tight or start to fall apart on the field, their mental game quickly falls apart too. Players choke. Performance suffers. The key, then, is not to have a false sense of security, but make developing *real* mental toughness a priority.

Tim Corbin, the head baseball coach at Vanderbilt University, does an interesting demonstration for incoming recruits (Schwartz, 2008). He puts a flame to a marshmallow, a jelly bean, and a rock. The marshmallow represents a player who has no mental game at all. When the heat is on, he quickly melts. The jelly bean is the player who only seems to have a good mental game. When things are going well, his mental game is solid. However, when the heat gets turned up, he too, melts. Now, the rock is the player who has a great mental approach. When the heat is turned up, he doesn't melt. His approach is consistently tough. Not easily shaken, he is able to stay focused and confident. He plays each game one pitch at a time. We want players who are rocks!

This book will help you change your mental approach to the game of baseball. You will gain an appreciation for true mental toughness on the baseball field. In Part I of the book, you will learn how to build what I call, the "mentally tough personality." This type of personality is at the "core" of mentally tough athletes. It becomes part of them and transforms the way they feel, think about, and behave in relationship to their sport. The mentally tough personality is multidimensional and takes work to develop.

We will start the process by building it piece by piece. The building blocks of a mentally tough personality include:
- Taking charge of your own development
- Setting goals

- Getting and staying motivated
- Learning to be *for yourself* rather than *against yourself*
- Playing arrows-out
- Effectively coping with failure
- Managing self-talk
- Sharpening concentration
- Conquering anxiety and controlling anger
- Establishing a reset mechanism by using a release
- Refining visualization skills
- Strengthening confidence and capitalizing on success

In Part II, you will learn how to put the mentally tough personality to work during actual game situations. A series of core beliefs about performance are explained. The goal, here, is to get you in the optimal mental state for the most important pitch of the game - - the very next one. This optimal state involves an effort to mimic being in the "zone," during what I call the "Instant of Performance," or "IOP." The Instant of Performance is the brief period of time that begins when both the pitcher and hitter are ready and ends when the ball reaches the plate. By intentionally completing a series of actions as part of a pre-pitch routine, you will learn what you should be feeling, thinking and doing during this critical period. While being in the optimal state of mind does not always guarantee success, this mental approach gives you the **best chance of success** on the most important pitch in any game - -the *very next one*.

So, you will learn not only *what to do*, but also *how to do it*. Read each section carefully and really think about the concepts. Make sure you complete each and every exercise. Keep in mind that, like practicing physical skills, there are no short-cuts, no magic wands, no secrets to developing a sound mental game. Mental skills training isn't about group hugs and high fives. It is about real techniques that require real effort.

Make a commitment to add regular mental skills practice to your baseball preparation. Top players have both a strong physical game and a great mental game. You can too.

Recap

1. Baseball is a mental game. Developing a sound mental game is critical to success.

2. Most players and teams do not spend enough time working on mental game skills.

3. Building a Mentally Tough Personality (MTP) is at the core of a great mental game. The process is explained in Part I of this book.

4. The MTP is achieved by developing a number of key skills that must be practiced. These components then become an automatic part of how a player thinks, feels and behaves when playing baseball.

5. Part II of the book focuses on the mental game and actual game performance. The Instant of Performance (IOP), the importance of routines, and the use of releases, when trying to mimic the zone, are all explained.

Sharpen Your Mental Game

1. Think of a player that you feel has mental toughness. Describe his attitude. How does he physically carry himself? How does he approach game day? How does he cope with failure? What is he thinking, feeling and doing in clutch situations?

2. Think about your mental game. What are your strengths? What are your weaknesses?

Chapter 2

You Are the Project

*"Always give 100 percent and you'll never
have to second guess yourself." ~ Tommy John*

In order to become a complete player, you must see
yourself as a project. Yes, becoming the best player possible is
now *your* mission. **You are the project.** As with any project,
you have to have a plan, a solid commitment to the plan, and the
willingness to work very hard to see it through. You make the
commitment and do the work. Keep in mind, some things might
seem awkward or clunky at first, but stick with it. Take your
mental game seriously – don't just "dabble" in the mental game.
After all, how good can you ever get at anything if you are just
dabbling?

Part of seeing yourself as a project is first understanding
that ultimately, you are the only one who can make yourself a
better player. Yes, *you* are responsible for your development.
Coaches, parents, and teammates can teach, challenge, and
support you, but how good you become is up to you. Players
can't rely on others to build up their mental game or blame
others for their lack of improvement. How good do you want to
be? How hard are you willing to work? Your answers will
determine your level of success.

As a baseball player, take charge and strive to *get better every day*. Before each practice, ask yourself, "What am I going to do today to become a better player?" Have a plan. Push yourself. Practice with intention. *You are really competing against yourself.*

In order to improve, players need to have an accurate view of their strengths and weaknesses. What do you do well? What do you need to work on? If you are not sure, ask! Talk to your coaches. Get some suggestions on exactly what you need to do to improve as a player.

Sometimes players let their egos get in the way. They are afraid to ask about, and work on, their weaknesses. It is much easier—and safer—to spend most of the time doing things they do well (e.g., hitting a waist high fastball). It is fun. It is easy. There isn't any ego risk.

Do not make this mistake. You must be willing to work on your weaknesses. If you can't hit the curve, work on it! If you struggle with bunting, work at it! If throwing a good change-up is giving you trouble, make it a priority in practice. Put your ego in the back pocket and take the risk. Again, understanding and working on weaknesses is part of the project of being the best player you can be.

Goal setting is also important. Karlene Sugarman (1999), in her book *Winning the Mental Way*, stresses the importance of effective goal setting. When asked, most players report having little trouble listing goals. "I want to hit 10 home runs." "I want to bat .390." "I want to win 15 games this year." These are called **outcome goals** because they are future-oriented and are not entirely under the player's control.

While outcome goals are common, and do provide a framework, players need **process goals** also. Think of process goals as being *steps* towards outcome goals. These goals are concrete things that you write down and clearly measure.

Process goals are important because they are more specific, immediate, and *under the athlete's control.* Focusing on process goals will help you achieve the outcome goals.

For example, if your outcome goal is to win 15 games this year, ask yourself what *exactly* you need to do in order to give yourself the best chance of making that happen. Asking yourself this question forces you to take a closer look at your strengths and weaknesses and to develop a plan of attack. So, looking back at last season, you realize for example that you tired quickly and lost both velocity and control as the game progressed. To address these issues, you now set a goal to get in better physical condition by lifting three times per week, running 20 minutes of wind sprints at least three times per week, and eating healthier. For hitters, the outcome goal of hitting .390 might involve several process goals such as lifting weights three times per week, spending an extra 25 minutes, three times a week hitting curveballs, and treating the last 10 swings of batting practice as if they were real-game situations. It is important to write down these process goals and chart your progress.

Begin your goal setting with long-term outcome goals, followed by a critical analysis of what process goals you will use to guide your progress.

Suggestions for Goal Setting

1. Include both outcome and process goals.
2. Use positive statements and list specific, measurable goals.
3. Write your goals down and develop a specific plan as to how, when, and where you will take steps to achieve them.
4. Chart your progress and keep this chart in a very public place.

5. Reward yourself for meeting your daily goals. Take
    pride in your accomplishments!

(Adapted from *Winning the Mental Way* (Sugarman,
1999).

Once you have set your goals, it is important to consider
your level of motivation. Motivation is a critical part of the MTP.
Defining your goals is of little value without motivation and hard
work. Motivation is the drive that pushes you to excel. Again,
coaches and teammates can help motivate you, but elite athletes
are *self-motivated*. They are driven. They want to compete.
They want to win.

What if you simply can't get motivated? From time to
time, everyone finds it difficult to find motivation. You just don't
feel like doing the things that need to get done. Do not fall into
the trap of "waiting to get motivated." If you wait, the
motivation may never come. Instead of waiting for motivation to
magically happen, you may need to prime the pump by taking
some action *first*. Action leads to motivation, which leads to
more action.

Action ⟶ **Motivation** ⟶ **More Action**

For example, if you do not feel like going to the weight
room to work out, do not wait for the motivation to come, because
it may not. Instead, get your clothes changed. Get yourself to
the weight room and begin your workout, even if you do not feel
like it. You will find that your initial actions (getting changed,
getting to the weight room, and starting to lift) will lead to
motivation to take further action and you will complete the
workout.

What if motivation wanes during the workout? Here are
several suggestions:

First, you must choose to have a strong work ethic. Choose? Is having a strong work ethic a choice? Yes. Not only is a strong work ethic a choice, but it is another key ingredient in the mentally tough personality. Elite athletes, even though they are blessed with physical talent, work hard to get better. Like these athletes, you need to make a commitment to work hard. Never let anyone outwork you. You will be playing against players and teams that are working very hard to get better. They are pushing themselves, individually and as a team, *so that they can beat you!* They want to be the ones walking off the field as winners, with high fives and big smiles. Outwork them! Never let anyone outwork you.

If motivation is fading and you are feeling like quitting, another technique to try is to use "the five more rule." Push yourself to do five more repetitions, five more minutes on the treadmill, or five more wind sprints. When you're finished, applaud yourself for the great work!

Finally, develop a set of verbal and behavioral "cues" that you can use to push yourself harder during workouts. To do this, think of an athlete who is incredibly dedicated and hardworking. Imagine his workout. This is now your "role model." Think of a word or short phrase to instantly bring up an image of this athlete. When you are tired and feel like giving up during a workout, you will use this quick verbal cue to push yourself further. Also, develop a quick behavioral cue to serve as a reminder of this athlete's hard work and how you want to emulate it. This can be as simple as a pinch of a finger or a slap on the leg. It doesn't have to be elaborate or obvious to anyone. It is your own signal to refocus, suck it up and push harder. Remember: use positive self-talk to give yourself credit after each great workout.

In addition to working hard during individual workouts, players must view team practices as valuable. Too often, players view practice as a hassle, a necessary evil, a complete drudgery. Because they fail to see the value of practice, players lose focus, do drills half-heartedly (when they can get away with it), and even try to find excuses to miss practice.

After being fined for missing practice, NBA guard Allen Iverson launched into his now famous rant ("Iverson practice!," 2006) . During a news conference he said, "Hey I hear you. It's funny to me too. Hey it's strange to me too, but we're talking about practice man! We're not even talking about the game when it actually matters. We're talking about practice!" One will never know just how much better this physically gifted athlete, and the teams he played for, could have been had he seen the value of practice.

If you are truly driven to reach your physical and mental peak as a baseball player, you must take a different perspective. Do not fall into the trap of seeing practice as something you do for the coach, for your parents or simply because you *have to do it*. See practice, instead, as *your opportunity* to get better. Practice is for you!

Practice is valuable for a number of important reasons. First, it helps build muscle memory. This is critical because at the Instant of Performance, you want to trust your body completely. You must be able to instantaneously react with the optimal motor responses. There is no time to think. Muscle memory, which is learned through repetition, automatically guides performance. Baseball players rely heavily on muscle memory to perform at the highest skill level. To illustrate how muscle memory works, try writing your name as you usually do. Now, do it but think about it this time. What did you notice? There is hesitation and it is more difficult. The same is true when playing an action video game, a musical instrument, or shooting a free throw. All of these behaviors rely on well-developed muscle memory. Think and you are done!

Practice is also important because it provides players with a "mental memory" of different situations. For example, the more often you see a curveball or bad hop ground ball, the more likely you will mentally react efficiently. This is because when humans are faced with a new situation, there is often a split second of hesitation. The brain sizes up the new situation and figures out what to do. Repeatedly experiencing situations in practice builds memories which allow for more automatic reactions during actual game performance. Simply put, the brain has seen it before and reacts without hesitation. This lack of hesitation could be the difference in hitting the baseball or not, fielding the hot grounder or turning and watching your outfielder picking it up.

Preparation for practice is vital. Unfortunately, few players are aware of just how important it is to take some time and quietly think about the upcoming practice. Mentally prepare to have a great practice by focusing on how you plan to give maximum effort to each drill, considering which skills you may want to emphasize, and visualizing yourself playing well during practice. Finally, get energized and emotionally excited about playing baseball!

Building the MTP begins by seeing yourself as a project. Take charge of your development. Get an accurate view of strengths and weakness; set specific goals; and stay motivated to work hard at achieving them. Take practices seriously and spend time mentally preparing yourself to get the most out of your practice time. Remember, all of these things are within your control. **You are the project.**

Recap

1. See yourself as a project. You are ultimately in charge of your own player development. You are the project manager.
2. Projects start with a plan followed by strong commitment and hard work. Your baseball career is no different.
3. Setting goals, both outcome and process, are critical to your development. Outcome goals are broad and future-oriented goals that provide a framework for success. Process goals are immediate, clear, specific, and measurable.
4. Stay motivated, and remember: Sometimes it takes initial action to create motivation.
5. If motivation begins to fade during workouts or practice use the five more rule, an empowering personal slogan and a behavioral cue to stay motivated instead of quitting.
6. Practice is important. Value it. It is your opportunity to get better! Spend time before each practice getting mentally prepared to play your best.

Sharpen Your Mental Game

1. Complete a list of outcome and process goals. Print out calendar and chart progress.

2. Think of the hardest working athlete you can. Visualize him working hard, even when he is exhausted. Write down what he must be thinking to get and stay motivated.

3. Write down a personal slogan that will remind you of this
   role model. Write down a quick and simple behavioral cue
   (i.e., snapping your fingers, tapping your leg, etc.) that you
   will use to remind you of his/her work ethic. Make sure you
   practice this during your next workout.

Chapter 3

Are You For Yourself or Against Yourself?

"If you learn to like yourself, you will always have a best friend.
Sometimes in baseball, you really need a best friend."
~ Ickes

Are you for yourself or against yourself? Newman and Berkowitz (1986) ask this very powerful question in their book *How to Be Your Own Best Friend*. At first glance, many people say, "Why, of course I am for myself." But are they? Are you? Being for yourself means that each thought and each action is productive, enhancing, and growth-oriented. Becoming aware of your mistakes and working hard to improve is an example of a **for yourself** action. If you are thinking and doing things that make you a better person and a better player, you are for yourself.

The flip side of that coin, being against yourself, means that you say and do things, often automatically, that are self-defeating. Believing negative self-talk without question is a common example of an **against yourself** action. Continuing bad habits is yet another example.

How does that happen? People are smart, right? People want to be happy, right? People want to succeed, right? Often, being against yourself boils down to not being aware of what you are thinking and doing, as if your thoughts and actions are on automatic pilot. The same thoughts and actions, even though negative, just seem to flow without any checks or balances. Players get in the trap of unchecked negative self-talk when they automatically doubt their ability after failure or automatically get anxious in clutch situations. Awareness is the first step in determining if what you are thinking and doing falls into the category of *for yourself* or *against yourself*.

Sometimes, unfortunately, players are aware that their actions and thoughts are self-defeating, but they repeat the same actions. People take the path of least resistance. As a clinical psychologist, I often see *against yourself* behaviors in clients' relationships with other people, food, alcohol, drugs, work, and issues related to real self-improvement. Even if clients *know* that the way they think and how they behave are destructive, they continue to do it.

It is easier to continue in an unfulfilling relationship than to take the risk to try and fix it. It is easier to eat that extra piece of cake than to say no and stick to a healthy diet. It is easier to self-medicate with drugs, alcohol, and cigarettes than to address real frustrations, hurts, and current problems. It is easier to bury oneself in work than to look at other things. It is easier to sit on the couch than to exercise. It is easier to continue to beat yourself up emotionally than to change your thinking.

Baseball players fall into the same trap. Even if they know what they are thinking or doing isn't helpful, they continue to do it. Self-defeating thoughts just seem natural, and in many ways, they are. Albert Ellis (1975), in the book *The New Guide to Rational Living*, tells us that negative thinking is the natural state, and that we must continually be aware of our thoughts, rationally challenge them, and replace negative thinking with more realistic and adaptive thoughts.

Deciding that you are truly *for yourself* rather than *against yourself* is at the core of the mentally tough personality. Players must train themselves to process all thoughts and actions through this critical filter: "Am I for myself or against myself?" *Make a commitment to think and do only those things that make you a better player.* Sometimes, choosing to improve yourself as a player means taking the tougher route. Working out, eating right, spending time on the mental game, listening and following coaches' instructions are examples of doing *for yourself* actions.

Once you have determined that you need to change unproductive thoughts and behaviors, commit to change, and commit to changing right now! A major trap for most people is delaying efforts to change. "I'll start working out tomorrow. I'll eat healthier beginning next month. I'll quit smoking when things are not as stressful, maybe next year." Sadly, tomorrow, next month, and next year often come and go without seeing any change. The simple act of delaying change prevents most change from happening. At the end of this chapter there is an exercise that involves listing *against yourself* behaviors that you would like to change. Commit to making those changes immediately!

So, pay attention to yourself. Continually ask yourself this key question: "Am I for myself or against myself?" If you find thoughts and actions that are self-defeating, list productive alternatives, and *choose* to consciously change your path. Commit to being *for yourself* from this moment forward.

Recap

1. Players need to constantly be aware of what they are thinking and doing. These thoughts and actions must be evaluated as being *for yourself* or *against yourself*. *For yourself* thoughts and actions are those that lead to personal growth. *Against yourself* actions are those that hurt performance and prevent progress.

2. Sometimes players continue to have detrimental thoughts and behaviors due to a lack of awareness. They think and do things out of habit without reflecting on exactly what they are thinking and doing.

3. Still other people may know that they are engaging in *against yourself* thoughts and behaviors, but continue to do them anyway. Awareness must be followed by a commitment to change self-defeating thoughts and behaviors.

4. Commit to change self-defeating thoughts and behaviors immediately. Delaying change is a trap. Do it right now!

Sharpen Your Mental Game

1. Jot down a quick list of things players think and do that are clearly "against themselves."

2. List things that you think or do that do not help your chances of success. Circle those things that you are willing to commit to changing right now! Remember to periodically do a self-check, and do not forget to give yourself credit for success.

3. List *for yourself* thoughts and behaviors that you are doing right now. Write down specific examples of when *for yourself* behaviors have helped you succeed during a game.

Chapter 4

Playing Arrows-Out

"Are you crying? Are you crying? ARE YOU CRYING? There's no crying, there's no crying in baseball. ~ Tom Hanks, as Jimmy Dugan (A League of Their Own. 1992).

One of the most important concepts that I teach players is the importance of playing with an arrows-out attitude. Dr. Tom Hanson (2008) describes it as an energy flow that points outward from the player. Imagine an arrow of energy that points towards others, the field, and the ball. Arrow-out players exude confidence, control, and tough-mindedness. Dr. Hanson uses Derek Jeter as a prime example of an arrows-out player. Jeter directs his energy outward and carries himself in this confident manner, no matter what the situation. Arrows-out is the positive direction, the direction of confidence.

Dr. Hanson also describes players who have their energy arrows pointing back towards themselves. Their thoughts and actions are all about them. He stated that arrows-in players ask questions like: "What about me? What does the coach think of me? What are my statistics? Aren't I something?" When they are in a slump, arrows-in players say things like "I can't hit. I suck." The focus is on them, not on the opponent and not on their team.

Expanding on Dr. Hanson's concept of arrows-out versus arrows-in, I like players to think of their attitude as being that of either a gamer (arrows-out) or a victim (arrows-in). Gamers exhibit the arrows-out attitude by being confident, tough, and resilient. They take it to the opponent every pitch, no matter what the score, no matter what the situation. Playing arrows-out is to play baseball with a dogged determination. When bad things happen (i.e., striking out, making an error, etc.), gamers pick themselves up and get right back in the game.

Victims, on the other hand, play arrows-in. All the energy arrows are pointing back at them. They feel weak, helpless, and small. Arrows-in players lack confidence and predict failure. Arrows-in players see themselves as victims of fate saying things like, "Did you see that umpire's call? I can't believe I hit that hard shot and he caught it. I'll never hit this pitcher." They have a "poor-me" attitude. These players mope around. They seek attention and pity from coaches, teammates, fans, and family members. If things don't go well on the field, they whine, they lose energy, their shoulders sag, and physically carry themselves in a defeated manner. Sometimes they cry, but there is no crying in baseball!

Coaches and teammates do not want victims. They want gamers. Being a victim (arrows-in) does not give you the best chance of success on the very next pitch. Arrows-in baseball does not give your team the best chance of success.

Playing arrows-out is contagious. When individual players chose to play with this attitude, soon the entire team begins to play this way. An arrows-out team is a much more difficult opponent to defeat.

I really like the distinction of being an arrow-out or arrows-in player. Top players have an arrows-out attitude. When I work with individual players and with teams, I emphasize that mentally tough players always play arrows-out.

They fight the urge to focus on themselves. They refuse to *choose* to play arrows-in. Yes, it is a *choice*.

Your mission, as part of building a MTP, is to always pay attention to whether you are playing arrows-out or arrows-in. If you find yourself feeling like a victim, immediately *make a choice* to change that attitude. Do not allow yourself to play arrows-in one minute longer. Playing arrows-out will help you perform better and will also earn a great deal more respect from coaches, teammates, and opponents. Starting right now, commit to becoming an arrows-out player.

Recap

1. Players need to play arrows-out baseball, not arrows-in. Arrows-out means the focus of energy is moving from you and not towards you. Arrows-out means taking charge. Playing arrows-out is a *choice*.

2. Arrows-out players are gamers, not victims. They do not get caught up in whining and crying if things do not go well. Instead, they accept the challenges with a sense of determination and resolve.

3. As more and more players adopt an arrows-out attitude, the team attitude becomes arrows-out and the team becomes much more difficult to defeat.

Sharpen Your Mental Game

1. Write down examples of when you played arrows-in baseball.
    Write down specifically what you thought, felt, and did. List
    game situations that sometimes trigger arrows-in feelings for
    you.

2. List arrows-out performances you have witnessed in person
    or on television. Describe the athlete's actions and emotions.

3. Discuss times when you have played arrows-out. How does it
    feel playing arrows-out? Comment on the difference in your
    performance when you approached the game arrows-out
    versus when you played arrows-in.

Chapter 5

Understanding Failure

"Failure doesn't have to be your friend, but you must learn to at least be in the same room together."
~ Ickes

The mentally tough player understands the reality of failure and the importance of keeping it in perspective. This chapter will focus on gaining a better understanding of the role failure plays in the game of baseball. You will also learn how to realistically define failure. Finally, you will learn how to develop strategies to effectively conquer the fear of failure.

Baseball is a Game of Failure

It has been said many times by players, managers, and sport psychologists: Baseball is a game of failure. Players *fail most of the time.* In professional baseball, if someone hit .350 over the course of a long career, he goes into the Hall of Fame. He is a great hitter who "failed" 650 out of 1000 at bats.

Failure is simply part of the game of baseball. Period. It is going to happen. It is a reality. Robert Ringer (1977), in his book *Looking Out For Number One*, tells us that reality isn't what we hope it is or want it to be, but reality is reality. So, it is important to accept the risk that, despite your best efforts, you will sometimes fail. The mentally tough athlete understands this reality and is not completely devastated when failure occurs.

You must keep failure in perspective. Be careful not to see failure as catastrophic. I have worked with players who have a difficult time coping with failing because they believe if they fail, the world might stop spinning. Talk about pressure! Fearing failure increases anxiety and hurts performance. All players want to succeed. No one likes to fail. But, again, failure sometimes happens. Put forth your maximum effort and respect the outcome.

It is also critical to remember that one failure does not mean that you will always fail. This is another common trap. Some players immediately lose confidence if they strike out in their first at bat in a game. Predicting failure hurts performance! It is critical to understand that each pitch is another opportunity to succeed.

Players Cannot Completely Control Success and Failure

Baseball players also must realize that they do not have complete control over success and failure. In other sports, players have more control as there are fewer outside variables to interfere with performance. Think about a basketball player shooting a free throw or a golfer trying to sink a 3-foot putt. Both athletes have a great deal of control over success and failure. They are in charge. If they have practiced and do everything right, they will succeed.

In baseball, players can do everything exactly right, and still "fail." For example, a pitcher may throw the perfect pitch and the batter hits a bloop single. A hitter may make the perfect swing and rip a line drive right at the third baseman. Players mistakenly view these situations as failures. They begin to question their ability and may fall into the trap of playing *arrows-in* baseball (e.g., poor me).

In the above examples did the pitcher or the hitter really fail? It is a common error to answer yes, merely based on the outcome. This is erroneous thinking! They are not actual failures. The players did exactly what they needed to do. They succeeded in their preparation and execution. Do not fall into the trap of defining failure solely based on outcomes. The mentally tough player always looks at performance in terms of process (what they did) versus outcome (what they ultimately have less control over). Evaluate preparation, effort, and execution (things you can control) rather than the outcome.

The Pace of the Game and Failure

By nature, baseball is a slow-paced game. Unlike basketball or football, baseball players have much more time to reflect on performance. If a player has a poor at-bat, it may be 20 or 30 minutes before he gets an opportunity to "redeem" himself. Pitchers who are taken out of the game wait even longer for another chance to succeed.

In the meantime, this period of time allows for negative self-talk to creep in and erode confidence. It is quite natural for players to ruminate about their poor performance. Players beat themselves up. They replay the failure over and over in their mind. I am sure this has happened to you. *Replaying failure will not help you play better!*

The key mental toughness skill is to develop a keen awareness of this negative self-talk and stop it immediately. Think about the lesson but let go of the negative emotion. No *arrows-in* baseball allowed! Use positive self-talk to make sure you treat yourself as you would treat your best friend. For example, if your friend makes an error or strikes out, you would probably say something like, "Shake it off. You'll get it the next time." Make the same type of statement to yourself. Also, instead of replaying the failure, spend this down-time thinking about how great it will feel when you succeed next time.

Players Tend to Focus on Failure

Players tend to focus on failure. For example, imagine that in a game you were 3 for 3 with a double and 4 RBI. However, in the last inning you are at-bat with the tying run on second and two outs. You strike out! What do you think you are thinking about as you gather your equipment? How about on the ride home, the rest of that night and when you wake up the next day? You would probably be thinking about failing during your last at-bat instead of the great at-bats you had earlier. This tendency must change. Focus, instead, on the successes such as the good swings you made or great fielding plays. *Focusing on failure, while automatic, will not help you play better.*

Failing on the Field is Not Failing as a Person

One of the most dangerous things a player can do is to intertwine self-worth and baseball performance. Baseball is a game. Baseball is part of your life. *It is not who you are.* There are many examples of great baseball players who were not viewed as good people. Should players be proud of their accomplishments? Yes, of course. However, do not equate your value as a person with how well you can pitch or hit a baseball. You are not *how* you play!

Recap

1. Baseball is a game of failure. It is important to keep failure in perspective. While no one likes to fail, it will happen sometimes. Failure must not be seen as catastrophic, as this will increase anxiety and hurt performance. Do not automatically predict that because of one bad at-bat or one bad pitch you will always fail.

2. Baseball players do not have complete control over the outcome. Good pitches get hit and great hits get caught. Focus on what you can control which is the process of being prepared for each pitch.

3. The pace of the game of baseball can make coping with failure extra difficult. Unlike other sports, there is a great deal of downtime between at-bats or pitching outings. Be careful not to fall into the trap of beating yourself up during this period of time.

4. Players tend to focus on failure. Make it a priority to become aware of this natural tendency and, instead, focus on successes. Remember what you did well!

5. Failing on the field does not mean you are a failure as a person. Your value as a person is not determined by how well you pitch or hit a baseball.

Sharpen Your Mental Game

1. Write a paragraph or two about how you plan to view failure more realistically from this point forward.

2. List all of things that you cannot control during a baseball
    game (i.e., weather, umpires, etc.). Now, list what you *can*
    control (i.e., attitude, preparation, etc.). Review your list and
    remind yourself to focus your time and energy on what you
    can control and not those things that you cannot.

3. Write a plan about how you will cope with failure during the downtime of a game or between games. Remember to intentionally replay past successes as part of your plan.

4. Write a paragraph or two about how, even though you love baseball, it is part of your life and not who you are as a person. List a few baseball players who are great on the field but not so great off the field. Then, list some players who are not superstars on the field, but are quality people.

Chapter 6

The Heckler in Your Head

"It's not what happens to you,
but how you react to it that matters."
~ Epictetus

Thousands of times every day you hear voices in your head. No, it isn't psychosis, but normal self-talk. Self-talk refers to internal verbalizations of our thoughts. Scientists estimate that the average person processes tens of thousands of self-talk statements per day. These thoughts and statements are automatic and help direct behavior (What do I want to wear?), evaluate experience (That pizza tasted like cardboard.), and evaluate ourselves (I did a good job on that project.). Our self-talk helps us survive (I better make sure to look both ways before crossing the street.). What you say to yourself has a powerful effect on what you feel and how you behave.

In baseball, becoming aware and making necessary adjustments to this self-talk is at the root of building and maintaining confidence. Sport psychologists teach players to evaluate self-talk in terms of being positive or negative. Positive self-talk is encouraging, confidence-boosting, and productive. Negative self-talk, on the other hand, is discouraging, confidence-eroding, and destructive.

All players experience negative self-talk. Those players with a MTP are aware of these unproductive thoughts and quickly make a choice to change to productive thinking. Unfortunately, many other players believe these persistent negative thoughts to be accurate. For example, when facing a tough pitcher, the MTP has self-talk that might sound like this, "He is good, but I can rip him." The player with negative self-talk might say, "This pitcher is too tough. I will probably strike out. I hope not, but he is better than I am." Which player do you think has the best chance of success on the very next pitch?

The following are the Rules of Self-Talk

1. Negative self-talk is normal but does not help you play better. This type of self-talk is not just unwanted or unacceptable, it is *toxic*! Negative thoughts must be viewed as poison and *must be completely eliminated*. Eliminating negative thoughts can be difficult at first, but becomes easier with awareness and practice. No negative self-talk allowed!

2. The first step towards more productive thinking is to understand that what you tell yourself is a *choice*. Even if it seems automatic, you have a choice as to whether or not you want to listen to, or change, this negative self-talk. Mentally tough players *make a choice* to think productive thoughts instead of unproductive ones.

3. The second step is to become aware of what you are thinking. What are you telling yourself? Think about times when you have lacked confidence or felt anxious during practice or a game. Pay close attention to your thoughts. On a piece of paper, make two columns. In the first column, write down these negative self-statements. In the second column, write down a positive counter-thought. After repeatedly doing this exercise on paper,

you will be able to simply do it in your head, in real-time. Changing negative self-talk takes a strong commitment to change and a great deal of practice.

4. Make sure self-statements are expressing what you *should do,* not what you *shouldn't do.* For example, a pitcher should say "hit your spot" rather than "don't walk him." For a hitter it might be "hit the ball hard" instead of "don't strike out."

5. Instead of focusing self-talk on failure, make sure to spend time focusing on what you do well. Spend time re-living your best performances. Enjoy it. Feel it. Tell yourself that you did a great job!

6. Develop a confidence boosting saying. I call this silent bragging, and it is a great technique. Not only is it perfectly fine to do, but it is vital to achieving peak performance. Have something you tell yourself on deck or as you are walking to the plate. It can be anything that helps you feel powerful, successful, and excited to hit. Some examples I have heard include:

   - "Nobody better!"
   - "It is ripping time!"
   - "I won't be denied!"
   - "Here comes my line shot!"
   - "Best hitter in the league!"
   - "Smoke it by him!"
   - "Right where I want it!"
   - "He can't touch this pitch!"

You must believe in yourself and a personal slogan helps reinforce and remind you of this belief.

7. Finally, *you must never say anything to yourself that you would not say to your very best friend.* Think about the last time you made an error or struck out. Pitchers, think

about the last time you walked a batter or gave up a big hit. What did you say to yourself? My guess is that your self-talk was pretty harsh. Now imagine that your very best friend just struck out in a clutch situation or gave up a big hit. He is coming back into the dugout, obviously disappointed. What would you say to him? Notice the difference? Most players are far more critical and harsh when they fail than they are when their friends fail. You need to be your own best friend. You must never say anything to yourself that you would not say to your friend.

Recap

1. Every day our minds generate thousands of thoughts and self-statements. This self-talk determines how we feel and what we do. While these productive thoughts are vital for survival, sometimes thoughts are nonproductive, meaning that they lead to decreased confidence and increased anxiety.

2. Negative self-talk hurts performance. All players experience this type of thinking from time to time, but mentally tough players have zero tolerance for negative self-talk. Through awareness and practice, they train themselves to *quickly* dismiss this type of thinking.

3. Understanding the danger of negative self-talk is just the first step. Knowing that you can actually change these thoughts is the second. Developing a keen awareness of what you are thinking is step three. Finally, actively challenging these negative thoughts and replacing them with positive alternatives is the last step. With practice, your awareness of and ability to challenge negative thinking becomes automatic.

4. Players need to make sure that they spend time thinking about successes instead of the natural tendency to focus on failures.

5. Make sure that your self-statements focus on what you want to do rather than on what you are trying to avoid doing.

6. Develop a confidence-boosting statement. Use this self-talk to gain a sense of power and excitement. This is called silent bragging and it is an effective part of having a great mental game.

7. Finally, never say anything to yourself that you would not say to your very best friend.

Sharpen Your Mental Game

1. Create 3 columns below. In column 1, write down *exactly* what you said to yourself after a poor performance. Do not sugar-coat it but write all of the self-statements in the exact language you used. In column 2, put a check mark by those statements that you would honestly say to your best friend as he was walking off the field following a rough outing. In column 3, write a positive self-statement to challenge your initial negative self-talk.

2. Write down a personal slogan that you will want to use
    for an instant confidence booster. Your slogan includes
    some form of silent bragging, reminding yourself that you
    are a good player. Some players write an acronym or
    some type of symbol on the inside of their hat, glove or
    shoe to serve as a reminder.

3. It is very important that you talk to yourself the same way you would talk to your best friend. With this in mind, write down some phrases that you will say to yourself whenever things do not go well.

4. Make a commitment to squelch all negative thinking. Over the next several weeks, pay attention to your self-talk. Whenever it is negative, write the thought down and then write a positive, competing thought beside it. If you work hard at developing zero tolerance for negative self-talk, your play will surely improve.

Chapter 7

To Think or Not to Think...

"This is baseball, not chess."
~ Ickes

Thinking while playing baseball is a complex topic. In the previous chapter we learned about self-talk and controlling *what you think*. In this chapter, the focus is on *when to think*. If you ask most players, they will tell you that when playing baseball, you should be thinking all of the time, that there should be a constant stream of thought. This is *not* the case. There is a time to think and a time to have a quiet mind. Controlling *when you think* is a critical skill.

Do not view baseball as a game where success is achieved by constantly thinking, analyzing, and evaluating. While thinking is important between pitches, the goal is to have zero conscious thoughts during the Instant of Performance. Consider what it is like when you are in the "zone." Are you thinking a great deal or is your mind quiet? Are you telling your body what to do or just letting your body react? Everything is on automatic pilot, isn't it? *You just play.* There is no self-awareness or conscious thought. It is just you and the baseball, complete concentration. The goal, then, is to *learn to think less*, during performance and thus, mimic "the zone."

Brain activation studies clearly demonstrate that top players actually have fewer thoughts during the Instant of Performance. Dr. Roland Carlstedt (2004) noted that during performance, top players have fewer conscious thoughts. These same players also exhibit a lower heart rate during the instant of performance. This heart deceleration is a marker for concentration. Below average players, on the other hand, will tend to think more and experience greater anxiety and thus, have higher heart rates. Fewer thoughts lead to less anxiety, greater focus, and an increased chance of success.

In the book, *Your Brain on Cubs: Inside the Heads of Players and Fans*, the author notes that professional hitters' brains respond differently to the pitch than those players with lesser ability (Gordon, 2008). Specifically, professional hitters activate only those areas of the brain that are required to hit, while lesser hitters have more brain activity, particularly in the areas associated with emotion. This *extra* thinking and feeling creates inefficiencies in both concentration and motor responses.

Dave Baldwin (2009), in the article *Unraveling the Batter's Brain*, writes that a batter hits with his unconscious mind. He discusses research conducted in the 1970's by neurophysiologist Benjamin Libet, who discovered that a batter's physical swing begins *before* conscious awareness. In other words, because a good fastball takes less than four-tenths of a second to reach the plate, there is no time to *think* about swinging. The swing relies on unconscious or automatic motor responses. Conscious thoughts impair this automatic process (Libet, 1985; Libet et.al., 1983).

In 1993, Dr. Tom Amberry, a retired podiatrist, set the world record for most consecutive basketball free throws at 2,750. Yes, 2,750! He shot free-throws for twelve hours and did not miss. He only quit because the gym was closing. In his book, *Free Throw* (1996), he talks about the importance of the mental game, including the need to have an empty mind during performance. On his website http://freethrow.com, he states, "When I shoot a free throw, I don't think of anything else. It is important to have the right mechanics. Once you learn to put your body in the proper position and shoot correctly, then the rest is mental." Dr. Amberry is talking about developing muscle memory during practices and then trusting your body to do what it is trained to do. During performance, no conscious thought is needed. In fact, thinking is likely to hurt performance!

The idea that performers should have fewer conscious thoughts is also supported by research involving professional musicians and professional video game players. Instead of increased brain activation, these skilled performers actually have fewer conscious thoughts and rely on muscle memory to guide performance. You may have experienced this type of muscle memory when playing video games that require quick reaction times (e.g., the various video guitar games). To perform well, it takes practice and building muscle memory. If you think, you are done!

You may also have experienced the effects of thinking too much while playing baseball. Players, particularly when in a slump, have racing thoughts or what is commonly called mental clutter. The focus turns to the internal—their own thoughts and feelings, rather than the external—the baseball. It is hard to concentrate. Anxiety increases. Performance suffers. Has this happened to you? How did you perform?

The primary goal is to *think when you should be thinking*, between pitches, and to *have zero thoughts during the instant of performance*. This is a key skill, whether you are a pitcher, fielder, or a hitter. Between pitches is the time to think about strategy; to develop a plan. What is the sign? What do I want to do with this next pitch? Are there reminders about my mechanics that I need to review? For hitters, this is the time to think about the count and, perhaps, sitting on a pitch. For pitchers, this is the time to think about pitch selection and location. Fielders, this is the time to get an overview of the game situation and put together a plan of action if the ball is hit to you. So, thinking is done between pitches and not during the instant of performance.

I have had some players express their concerns about turning thoughts off as they prepare for the instant of performance. "Won't I forget what I am supposed to do? Shouldn't I be reminding myself about mechanics when I am in the box? Wouldn't it be a good idea to pump myself up by saying something positive over and over while I am in the box or as I am starting my windup?" The answer to all of these questions is NO!

During performance, you must not coach nor cheerlead, as this only adds mental clutter. The goal is to have zero thoughts during the instant of performance. By reducing thinking, you are turning performance completely over to your body. Learn to trust yourself. You know how to pitch! You know how to hit! Pitchers, always do your thinking before you begin your motion. Hitters, always do your thinking outside of the box.

You might be saying, "Okay, Dr. Ickes, I get it no thinking during the instant of performance...but how can I stop thinking?" Most players have tried to simply tell themselves to quit thinking. As you know, telling yourself not to think about something is not very effective (e.g., whatever you do, do not think about a pink elephant). Instead, you must make use of an effective pre-pitch routine.

A pre-pitch routine is a series of well-practiced mental and physical activities that players automatically perform before each pitch. This routine sets the stage for optimal performance by reducing conscious thought, controlling negative emotions, instilling confidence, and improving focus and concentration.

(We will cover pre-pitch routines in greater detail in Chapter 13). One of the key components to a quality pre-pitch routine is learning how to shut-off conscious thoughts.

An effective technique that I teach involves the use of a focal point. A typical focal point is a small spot on the bat. Players can also choose to use a smudge on the plate, the same scuff on their shoe, or even an object in the distance. The key is not what you choose to focus on, but rather training yourself to quickly develop a deep focus on that spot. First, you must be relaxed. This is important because when humans concentrate, we have a natural tendency to tense up. Now, take a deep breath and then zero in on your focal point. Do not simply look at the focal point; study it, see the details. Do not try to analyze what you are seeing into words; just study it like you have never seen anything like it before. Allow your conscious thoughts to *drift* away rather than trying to *push* them away.

After studying the focal point briefly (you will get quicker and quicker with practice) your eyes then move to the pitcher's release point. It is important to avoid looking anywhere else between the focal point and release point, as to avoid distraction. If you do find yourself thinking, make sure to call time-out and re-set your routine.

With practice, you can train yourself to quickly stop consciously thinking. Your focus will shift from internal (your thoughts) to external (the baseball in space). There are many great examples of college and professional players using this technique. For example, a video clip of Pedro Alvarez using a focal point as part of his pre-pitch routine can be found at www.youtube.com ("Pedro Alvarez home," 2008).

Learning to turn off conscious thinking gives you the best chance of success. With practice, using your focal point becomes an automatic part of your game.

Recap

1. Brain activation studies clearly demonstrate that skilled performers actually have less brain activity during performance than less skilled players. Top players allow muscle memory to take the lead rather than conscious awareness.

2. Learning to control when you think is a critical skill. One useful technique is to make use of a focal point. This can be a small spot on your bat, shoe, or even home plate. As you step into the box, intensely focus on the spot, allowing all of your conscious thoughts to drift away. Your eyes move from the focal point directly to the pitcher's release point. The effective use of a focal point becomes automatic with practice.

3. Learning to control *when to think* is a critical skill. Baseball is not a game where success is achieved by a constant stream of thought. Instead, there is a time to think and a time (pre-performance) to have a quiet mind (during performance). Between pitches you must evaluate, analyze, and plan. However, during the instant of performance, conscious thought must stop.

Sharpen Your Mental Game

1.   Think back to specific situations when you were struggling
     or in a slump. Describe your thoughts during performance.
     What were you thinking? Where you thinking too much?
     What did you notice about the speed of the game and your
     performance?

2. Think back to specific situations when you were in the zone. Describe your thinking. What did you notice about the speed of the game and your performance?

3. Spend at least 5 minutes a day practicing shutting off your conscious thoughts by using a focal point. You may want to use a small spot on your baseball bat or baseball glove. Take a deep, relaxing breath and zero in on the details of the focal point. Do not try to put your observations into words, instead let your thoughts drift away. Remember, you only have to be thought-free for 3-5 seconds at a time. Write down what this experience was like and comment on the effects of repeatedly practicing this exercise.

Chapter 8

Improving Concentration

"If you chase two rabbits, both will escape."
~ Unknown

Concentration is vital to playing successful baseball. It is a skill that can be understood and developed through practice. Because baseball is a long game, players are sometimes prone to lapses in concentration. Also, players sometimes are easily distracted; that is, they are concentrating on the wrong things, rather than the task at hand. The mentally tough player masters the art of staying focused at the *right time* on the *right thing*.

When is *the right time*?

Baseball games can last 2 to 3 hours and during the game there is a great deal of downtime. Just like thinking, players cannot be expected to have laser-like focus the entire time. Instead, see concentration as occurring in short, intensive bursts. Between pitches, players must make effective use of this downtime to relax and save their mental energy for the critical period during the next pitch. I do not mean that a player simply goes to sleep, but there is a period of some relaxation. Once the pitch is about to be made, all players need to get into the routine of complete, laser-like focus on the action. A baseball game is a series of multiple short bursts of extreme concentration. Get into the habit of consciously recognizing when you need to be your sharpest.

What is *the right thing*?

Players are constantly required to pay attention to, and simultaneously process, a great deal of information about what is happening around them. Baseball, like all sports, is a game of shifting focus or concentration. Sometimes the focus must be global or broad, such as taking into account the game situation. Sometimes the focus must be very specific or narrow, such as picking up the spin of a pitched baseball. Sometimes the focus is internal, such as reminding yourself of a pitching or hitting mechanic. Sometimes the focus is external, such as getting your signs from the third base coach.

The key to success is being able to quickly shift focus to the task requirement at hand. This means that all of the other things that are going on around you fade into the background. Distraction is nothing more than having non-essential information blend with required information.

Robert Nideffer (1993), an expert in the area of concentration and sports, describes concentration as being a combination of two dimensions: Width (Broad vs. Narrow) and Direction (Internal vs. External). In his article *Concentration Training for Peak Performance*, he detailed these four specific types or combinations:

Broad Internal: Concentrating on your general feelings, thoughts, and body sensations. How are you feeling about today's game?

Broad External: Concentrating on the wider environment. For example, the game situation, the crowd, the coach's comments.

Narrow Internal: An awareness of specific thoughts, feelings and movements. For example, this would be an awareness of where your hands are or how your foot feels in the batter's box.

Narrow External: Concentrating on a very specific area outside yourself. For a pitcher, it may be a small spot on the catcher's mitt. For hitters, it will be the ball coming out of the pitcher's release point.

During the game, a player needs to use all of these areas of concentration and have the skill to *shift concentration* at the right time. For example, imagine a hitter comes to bat with a runner on second, no outs, and the score tied late in the game. Let's take a look at how this shift should occur.

- He will use **Broad Internal** to get a quick gauge as to how he is feeling in general. Is he anxious? Confident? If he is anxious, he might take a few deep breaths to slow himself down. If he is not feeling confident, he might engage in positive self-talk, which allows him to get into the optimal mental state.

- He will use **Broad External** to gather information about the game situation and strategy (e.g., hit the ball to the right side to move the runner).

- He will then shift to **Narrow Internal** to remind himself, specifically, of what he needs to do to successfully accomplish this plan (e.g., let the ball get deep).

- The player then makes the *most* important shift: **Narrow External**. Here, he uses his pre-pitch routine to lock in on the release point. The goal at the instant of performance is for the hitter to be in a state of 100% narrow external focus. Conscious thought (internal focus) stops. There must not be any self-awareness, cheerleading, or analysis. There must be zero awareness of the crowd, other players, or what might or might not happen if he does not succeed (broad external). The player must be in a state of complete *narrow external* focus. For pitchers, the focus is your target. For hitters, your focus is the pitcher's release point and the baseball coming out of that space.

Dr. Nideffer, using the analogy of the brain as a high speed camera, explains why *narrow external* focus is critical to successful performance. He suggests that you think of your brain as a high speed camera that takes 40 pictures a second. Imagine a pitch taking about one second to make its way to the plate. These 40 pictures provide instantaneous feedback about where the ball is in space. Your brain, because of your experience hitting, automatically calculates whether the pitch will be in the strike zone or not. If it is a strike and you want to swing, the brain determines where exactly to swing in order to make contact.

If you have 100% narrow external focus, you will see all 40 pictures. You will be getting all of the data! Players refer to this as *seeing the baseball*. If, on the other hand, you are distracted by things such as internal thoughts or broad external factors (e.g. crowd noise), you may only get 20 pictures. There will be gaps in perception. This is why the game seems to *speed up* when you are distracted and *slows down* when the focus is completely **Narrow External**. The goal, then, is to develop your ability to have keen *narrow external* focus during the instant of performance.

Become aware of anything that interferes with *narrow external* focus. Sometimes players will get into the bad habit of looking into the stands or into the dugout between pitches. Sometimes, well-meaning teammates, parents, and coaches bombard players with suggestions during an at-bat. Encouragement is fantastic but coaching during an at-bat is unlikely to improve performance because it can create mental distraction.

Remember, because it is a skill, concentration can be practiced and strengthened. Perhaps the best tool to develop narrow external focus during the instant of performance is to use a focal point (discussed in the previous chapter). This focal point serves as a reset button for a clear mind. Make sure you regularly practice getting into this optimal thought-free state.

Recap

1. Concentration is a key skill that can be improved with practice.

2. Baseball requires brief periods of intense concentration. Because a baseball game may last 2 to 3 hours, it is important to maintain the mental energy to concentrate during critical periods.

3. Dr. Nideffer explains that there are four types of concentration: **Broad Internal, Broad External, Narrow Internal and Narrow External**.

4. In order to succeed, players must be able to efficiently shift total concentration to the task at hand. For example, **Broad External** allows a player to accurately get a sign from the third base coach. **Narrow External** allows him to completely focus on the baseball as it heads towards home plate.

5. During the instant of performance, concentration must be 100% *narrow external*. This means that there is an absence of conscious thought. There is also an absence of distraction from outside or external factors (i.e., fans, other players, etc.).

6. It is important to practice developing your ability to quickly shift to 100% *narrow external* focus. This can be done by using a focal point and allowing conscious thoughts to clear. It is a major requirement of your pre-pitch routine.

Sharpen Your Mental Game

1. Practice concentrating on any common object around the house (i.e., a label on a box, a glass, an article of clothing, etc.). For one minute, really study the details of the object *without putting your thoughts into words.* Let your conscious thoughts drift away. Simply, study it as though you have never seen it before. Try concentrating on different objects. Continue practicing this type of concentration daily, shortening the time you focus on the object. Do the exercise now. List what object you used and describe what the experience was like. Keep a chart of how your experiences change with practice.

2. During the instant of performance, concentration
    must be 100% **narrow external**. Any internal
    thoughts or external distractions will hurt
    performance. Make a list below of things that distract
    you during this critical time. What is your plan to
    reduce this distraction?

3. When playing catch, you and your partner can
    practice your concentration skills. Take a deep
    breath, look at a focal point on your glove, and then
    move your eyes to his release point. See nothing but
    the ball. What do the seams look like? Can you see
    any scuffs? Watch it the entire way into your glove.
    This is an excellent pre-game concentration drill.

Chapter 9

Controlling Emotions

"Spanning the globe to bring you the constant variety of sport! The thrill of victory...and the agony of defeat! The human drama of athletic competition! This is ABC's Wide World of Sports!"

One of the great things about playing a sport is the wide range of emotions that players experience. Excitement, determination, anxiety, elation, devastation are just some of the powerful emotions that are expressed on the field. It is important for the mentally tough player to understand and control emotional states during performance. Anxiety and anger are two emotions, that when left unchecked, hurt performance.

Anxiety

I am sure there have been times when you have been anxious during a game. Remember what that felt like? Physically, your body goes into a fight or flight response. Your heart rate increases, breathing becomes shallow and quick, and muscle tension increases. Too much muscle tension creates motor skill inefficiency.

In addition to physical changes, psychological changes occur. Thoughts increase. These thoughts tend to be Broad <u>and</u> Narrow Internal, as well as Broad External. Remember, this is just the opposite of what we want to have happening at the instant of performance. In order to have the best chance of success at the instant of performance there must be *complete narrow external focus*.

Anxious players often experience racing thoughts and accompanying negative self-talk. By racing thoughts I mean that players jump from thought to thought. "I have to make sure my stance is right. Should I change bats? What if I don't get a hit here? I wonder if the coach has confidence in me. What is the pitcher thinking? What are the fans thinking? Do they think I can get a hit? This pitcher is tough. I am not sure I can hit off him. I have to get a hit, though. Okay, you can do it. I hope he doesn't throw me his curve. He has a lot of strikeouts today. Man, I need to get a hit."

All of these types of thoughts flood the hitter's mind and will add to anxiety, which leads to more thinking and more anxiety. It is a vicious cycle. As you have learned already, players perform best—and the game slows down—w hen there are fewer thoughts at the instant of performance. Therefore, reducing anxiety slows the number of thoughts, which gives you the best chance of success.

Players who are overly anxious tend to do one of two things, both of which impair performance. They either over-react or under-react. Examples of over-reactions would include such things as swinging early on a pitch that is in the dirt or throwing the ball away in a rush. An example of under-reaction would be freezing at the plate and watching a third strike pass right down the middle of home plate. High levels of anxiety disrupt the flow of your game.

Why do players get anxious? Anxiety comes from uncertainty or a lack of confidence. There is uneasiness about whether or not the player will succeed. Performance becomes scary rather than calming, unpredictable rather than predictable, a struggle rather than enjoyable.

In order to manage anxiety, players must first learn to gain physical control of the body. The best way to do this is to practice *deep breathing exercises*. Clinical and sport psychologists have endorsed the use of deep breathing as a quick and efficient way to slow the body down. Clinically, this technique is very useful in helping clients with phobias and panic attacks. Sport psychologists teach athletes, regardless of their sport, that learning to take deep calming breaths is a great way to reduce the physical feeling of anxiety. Pay close attention the next time you watch a Major League Baseball game. Watch both pitchers and hitters and you will see that between pitches, they will take at least one deep breath. It is critical that you learn this skill and continuously use it when you play.

Ken Ravizza and Tom Hanson (1998), in their classic text *Heads-Up Baseball: Playing One Pitch at a Time*, do an excellent job of explaining the importance of deep breathing and how to master it. They point out that stopping to take a few deep breaths serves a number of key purposes. First, breathing helps players get control of their physical body. It slows things down physically, which, in turn slows things down mentally. These authors also point out that taking a deep breath helps players focus on the present moment, instead of the last pitch or what might happen later. It is a signal that it is this pitch, right now, that matters. They also suggest that taking this deep breath can establish a sense of rhythm, energize a player when he is feeling sluggish, and get rid of negative thinking. Adding deep breathing to your game is a key part of having a mentally tough personality.

Ravizza and Hanson suggest that throughout the day, players practice taking deep breaths. Air is slowly drawn into the abdomen, held momentarily, and then exhaled through the mouth. When inhaling, the stomach moves away from the spine and when exhaling, the chest is relaxed. (I like to encourage players to allow their shoulders to sag just a bit on exhale). They suggest that this breathing exercise can be done while carrying out daily activities or by setting aside a specific time to practice. If you are setting aside time, the authors suggest you lie on your back in a quiet room. Slowly inhale, and your stomach, not your chest, rises. Inhale to a count of 10 and pay attention to your breathing. Momentarily hold the breath and then relax on exhale. This should be practiced 5 to 20 minutes, every day or every other day, according to Ravizza and Hanson. For more information, I would encourage you to read their book. Deep breathing is a vital tool to quickly gain control over the physical arousal caused by anxiety.

Besides controlling their breathing, I teach baseball players to change their thinking. Specifically, the goal is to engage in self-talk that intentionally changes or converts the type of emotion experienced. This idea is based on the concept of reciprocal inhibition. Introduced in the 1950's by a famous clinical psychologist Joseph Wolpe (1958), reciprocal inhibition proposes that one cannot experience opposite emotions at *the exact same moment in time.* For example, you cannot be happy and sad at the same time; be shy and assertive at the same time; or be anxious and calm at the exact same moment. The key, then, is to find competing emotions (those that inhibit anxiety) and use self-talk to experience those instead. Two such emotions are excitement and determination.

Excitement is an emotion that is energizing. I was watching a college basketball team before its first game of the season. Following warm-ups, the team lined up for the national anthem and I noticed that the players could not stand still. Now, ˙ know that it is common for players to move around a bit as they ˙⁺ to play, but this was different. They were *really* moving,

swaying, and bouncing up and down on their feet. I wondered,
Are they excited or are they anxious?

Even though both emotions can create a high level of
physical energy, there is a big difference in terms of what is
going on mentally. Excited players are looking forward to
playing and playing well. They can't wait. They are *feeling it*.
They are confident! Excited players also expect to play well.
Anxious players, on the other hand, have some doubt about the
game or how they will play. They are not quite sure what is
going to happen. They are hoping to play well, wanting to play
well, and thinking they might play well, but there is still some
uncertainty. So, even if there is a great deal of energy, there is a
big difference in the emotion behind it. *Players need to be
excited, not anxious.*

Imagine that you are in the middle of a game and facing a
very tough pitcher who is dominating your team. Even imagine
that he struck you out in your first at-bat. Now, as you are on
deck, it would be natural to have self-talk like, "I hope I can hit
him. What if he throws me that nasty curve? Man, he is tough.
I can't believe how he is striking everyone out today. I just hope
I can at least get the bat on it this time." You are defeated
before you even get in the batter's box. This type of negative
thinking, although common, undermines confidence and creates
anxiety. While you feel a great deal of nervous energy, you are
not excited to hit because you are anxious and a bit fearful. The
more intense the anxiety, the less likely you are to succeed.

What should you do? First, make sure you take your slow
deep breaths to slow your body down and to relax your muscles.
Then, work on converting the feelings of anxiety into the
competing emotions of excitement and determination. This is
accomplished by changing your thoughts, and your self-talk,
about the upcoming at-bat. Specifically, you must change your
view of the situation and your ability to succeed. Instead of

focusing on how tough the pitchers is and how you might fail, see this at-bat as a challenge. Tell yourself something like, "Sure, he is having a great day. Everyone is expecting him to get me out—everyone, but me! It is going to be great to rip a shot off of him. It is going to be so cool to do some damage here. I'm a tough hitter and he is going to find out how tough!"

Seeing the upcoming at-bat as a challenge, instead of something to be feared, automatically reduces anxiety. Notice the difference in the emotions. There is positive, arrows-out energy. You are more in control. You are determined. You are more excited about this *opportunity to hit*.

Anger

Baseball can be a very frustrating game! Failure is common. Allowing anger to get out of control hurts performance. I have seen this many times. A pitcher, angry about missing his spot on the two previous pitches, throws the next pitch right down the middle and the batter hits it out of the park. A hitter, angry at an umpire's call, swings at a pitch out of the strike zone and strikes out. A fielder, angry because of a poor at-bat, boots an easy grounder. Mentally tough players effectively deal with anger.

Players holding onto anger find themselves out of control and performance suffers. Believe it or not, I once saw a hitter continue to argue a first pitch strike the entire time he was at bat, including the whole time he was actually in the batter's box. After the first called strike, he swung at a ball in the dirt for strike two. Still arguing, he then swung at a pitch over his head for strike three. The player then proceeded to yell at the umpire saying, "You took the bat out of my hands," before throwing the bat to the ground and getting ejected. It was an interesting at-bat for sure. Unable to let go of the anger following the first pitch, he lost his focus. He lost his chance to succeed.

Not only does anger hurt your focus, but throwing a temper tantrum can actually *help* the other team in a number of ways. First, it can increase your opponent's level of confidence. Opposing players, particularly the pitcher, love to see someone who just made an out throw a fit. It gives them a great sense of satisfaction. It boosts their confidence. Seeing that type of anger gives the opposing team a greater sense of being in control. Your opponents feel they have you right where they want you! Second, throwing a tantrum can get your opponent's fans fired up. Opposing fans love to see you sweat! This is particularly true in big games when you are on the road. Finally, throwing a tantrum can send an arrows-in signal to the rest of your teammates. The message is "I can't do it." Remember, both arrows-in and arrows-out attitudes are contagious.

Will you be frustrated? Sure. Will you get angry at yourself for failing? Sure. The key is to learn to quickly let go of this anger without throwing a tantrum. There is no need to curse loudly, throw your helmet, or to pound your bat into the ground on your way back to the dugout. If you strike out, everyone already knows you are disappointed and frustrated. You do not need to put on a show. Players who tantrum look silly. Tantrums are for three year-olds who don't get their candy at the store. Players with a mentally tough personality refuse to throw tantrums. Tantrums simply do not help you play better.

One effective alternative to throwing a tantrum is to convert anger into a more productive emotion—determination. Mariano Rivera, the New York Yankee closer, is a great example of someone who effectively handles frustration. In the article, *The Confidence Man*, Buster Olney (2004) writes about his interview with Rivera and how the pitcher faces adversity. He writes, "Rivera does not scream or throw his hat or kick over water coolers; he won't give them the satisfaction." In response, Rivera is quoted as saying, "And I never will. Never. You can't

let them get to you. You have to be the same, no matter what."
Rivera goes on to say that he does not recall feeling threatened
by experiencing anxiety and self-doubt. "I've always loved the
competition. I am not afraid of it." Become more determined to
succeed the next time out. *This must be your focus.* This is what
will give you the best chance of success.

Another tool to use when you are frustrated and angry is
to follow what I call the 3-second rule. You can be angry, *without
the outward hysterics*, for only 3 seconds. Then let go of the
anger so that you can be ready for the most important pitch, the
very next one. It is important that there is no carry over from
pitch to pitch, at-bat to at-bat, or game to game. I think
mastering the 3-second rule, is one of the most important mental
game concepts that I teach.

If you strike out, express your frustration *to yourself,* take
a deep breath to release some physical tension, look out at the
pitcher, use self-talk—vowing to get him next time, and calmly
make your way back to the dugout *with your head up.* Pitchers
and fielders need to follow a similar pattern: acknowledge the
anger to yourself, take a deep breath, make a positive self-
statement and *always keep your head up.* Again, you do not want
to give the other team any sense of confidence with any outward
display of anger or frustration.

In addition to becoming more determined and strictly
adhering to the 3-second rule, you must develop a *personal
release.* A release is a sequence of thoughts and behaviors that
act as a reset button. This pattern gets rid of the anger and gets
you back to start—a fresh start. Various sport psychologists hold
different ideas regarding the exact nature of a release, but nearly
all agree on the value of this important mental skill.

While specific releases will vary from player to player, I
feel that all releases must include the following: At least one
slow, deep breath, a behavior that causes a break in the action,

and some type of cleansing behavior. By cleansing behavior, I mean something that *wipes away* the mistake or frustration. A release does not have to be elaborate or time-consuming, but it does have to be well-practiced, so that it becomes automatic in a game situation.

What do releases look like? Most of the pitchers I work with will take a deep breath when getting the ball back from the catcher, turn their back to the plate and walk off the back of the mound. Then, they will engage in some type of cleansing behavior such as rubbing up the baseball, taking off the hat and wiping the brow, or bending down to fix the pant legs on their uniform.

Fielders must also develop and practice a release. After making an error, it is important to reset in order to regain focus on the present and prevent any negative carry-over. Here, a player can take a slow deep breath, step back from the normal fielding position or even turn away from home plate. Then get rid of the frustration by picking up dirt or grass and tossing it away, smoothing the infield surface, or taking the glove off. Once the glove goes back on, you are reset and ready to go. Again, what specifically you choose to do is not important, as long as it includes a deep breath, a pause in the action, and a way to symbolically get rid of the frustration.

One player told me that after an error, he pictures the play and then sees that image on fire and it burns to nothing. He then mentally replays several great plays he has made in the past. This "burn and replace" technique is his release. He is now 100% ready for the next pitch.

What you do as a release is not important, as long as it is effective for you. It is very, very important that you develop and use your releases in practice. Think about what you can use as a release. Do some experimentation to find out what works best. The goal is to have this release become a part of your personality, a part of your game. A quality release allows you to give complete focus to the most important pitch, the next one you make.

During an at-bat, hitters do not need to use a release, per se. Instead, hitters make use of a pre-pitch routine to reset between pitches. This routine includes a slow deep breath and the use of a focal point to reset. The same exact routine is used between every pitch. Pre-pitch routines are discussed later in the book. A release, explained above, may be used after making an out, particularly after a strike out.

Being able to control your emotions during a baseball game is a very important mental game skill.   Spend time mastering the techniques discussed in this chapter.   By effectively reducing anxiety and defusing anger, you will be able to stay focused and play your best baseball.

Recap

1. Emotions are an important part of baseball. Learning to control negative emotions like anxiety and anger will help performance.
2. Anxiety is often caused by a lack of confidence and creates muscle tension, increased thinking, and hurts concentration.
3. Anxiety can be reduced by using deep breaths to slow down the body. Competing emotions, such as excitement and determination, also reduce anxiety.
4. Uncontrolled anger hurts performance by reducing focus on the task at hand. Tantrums do not help players play better and they may even help your opponent.
5. There are several techniques that can be used to defuse anger including: deep breathing, following the 3-second rule, and using a well-practiced release.
6. The goal of the release is to act as a reset button. This is important as players must avoid any type of negative carry over from pitch to pitch, at-bat to at-bat, or game to game. Releases are player-specific, but must include a deep breath, something that allows for a break in the action, and some type of behavior that wipes away the frustration.

Sharpen Your Mental Game

1. Think about a time when you have been anxious before or during a game. Describe what you were thinking and feeling. Based on what you have learned in this chapter, describe exactly what you would do differently in that same situation. Keep in mind the concepts of deep breathing, competing emotions, and self-talk.

2. Practice deep breathing. Take 3 or 4 slow deep breaths, paying attention to your relaxation when you exhale. What did you notice? Do this several times throughout the day, in practice, and in actual games. After you have used deep breathing in practice or games, make a list below of actual situations where it has been helpful.

3. Determination is a key emotion that counteracts both anxiety
   and anger. Make a list of your own personal determination
   statements that you can use when you play.

4. Create your releases. Write down what you will use as a reset button, every time you get frustrated or angry. Develop releases to use in the field, as well as when you are pitching or hitting. Make sure to include all of the key components. *Use these releases in practice so they become automatic!*

Chapter 10

Visualization: If You See It, You Will Believe It

"Visualize this thing that you want, see it, feel it, believe in it.
Make your mental blueprint and begin to build."
~ Robert Collier

Many athletes use visualization to improve performance. For simplicity's sake, I am going to refer to visualization, guided imagery, mental rehearsal, and imagined practice all as "visualization." This chapter will discuss the effectiveness of using visualization and provides some suggestions on how and when to use visualization successfully.

Does visualization work?

The answer is, when done correctly, yes! In the article, *Onwards with the Evolution of Imagery Research in Sport Psychology* (Short & Monsma, 2006), the authors note that over 200 research studies have been conducted regarding the role of visual imagery in sport settings. Anne Isaac (1992) is just one of the many researchers supporting the view that visualization is effective, regardless of the particular sport or the actual skill level of the athlete.

In his book, *The Brain That Changes Itself*, Norman Doidge (2007) details numerous studies that have confirmed the power of mental practice. For instance, Dr. Doidge describes one study (Yue & Cole, 1992) in which researchers randomly assigned subjects to one of two conditions. In the first group, subjects spent five days actually doing physical exercise to increase finger muscle strength. In the second group, subjects merely imagined exercising and imagined a voice shouting encouragement. At the end of the study, those who actually exercised increased strength by 30% and, remarkably, those that only imagined exercising gained 22%.

Dr. Doidge (2007) states:

> One reason we can change our brains simply by imagining is that, from a neuroscientific point of view, imagining an act and doing it are not as different as they sound. When people close their eyes and visualize a simple object, such as the letter *a*, the primary visual cortex lights up, just as it would if the subject were actually looking at the letter *a*. Brain scans show that in action and imagination many of the same parts of the brain are activated. That is why visualizing can improve performance. (pp. 203-204)

How to use visualization

Much has been written about specific ways to visualize or use guided imagery. Most sport psychologists suggest a process similar to the following:

1. Visualization should take place in a quiet or relaxed atmosphere. Some players prefer to visualize while listening to music while others do not. Try both and see which works best for you. Many players find that the best time to visualize is right before going to sleep.

2. Players should practice visualization daily. I recommend at least 5-10 minutes a day to start and

gradually building yourself up to 15-30 minutes. Your visualization sessions can be split up during the day.

3. Make use of all of your senses. Do not merely see yourself performing well, but smell the smells, hear the crowd and teammates. Totally immerse yourself in the experience.

4. Visualization can involve performing the skill in first person (through your eyes) or in the eyes of an observer (third person). Most researchers suggest you do both, but mastering the first person perspective is critical.

5. Repeatedly visualize a successful scene, making each run-through more detailed and clear. Make sure to emotionally *feel* your success!

6. There are numerous online videos to help you learn to use visualization effectively. Be sure to check out these sites.

When should I use visualization?

There are several settings in which the use of visual imagery will be beneficial.

1. Visual imagery can be used after working on a particular swing or pitching mechanic. If you are learning something new or trying to correct a mechanical flaw, spend time each day seeing yourself performing that skill flawlessly.

2. It is important to mentally rehearse, both throughout the day and, most importantly, once you reach the ballpark. Many players I work with set aside quiet time during warm-ups to visualize their upcoming performance. Visualize yourself making great plays, having those perfect swings, or making those exceptional pitches. By clearly seeing success

beforehand, you are priming the pump for actual success. See it, feel it, and believe it.

3. An area that is often overlooked is the use of visualization post-performance. It is very important for you to spend time replaying your successes. If you had a great at-bat during practice or a game, visualize it again and again. Instead of one base hit, you have the opportunity to program your brain with 30-40 base hits. This will help you unconsciously foster confidence.

Visualization can be a very powerful tool to improve performance. Like all mental game techniques, it takes effort to perfect this skill. If you initially struggle with using visual imagery, do not give up. Keep working on it!

Recap

1. Visualization is a technique that employs mental performance in order to enhance physical performance. The effectiveness of these techniques is strongly supported by numerous research studies.

2. Make visualization a daily part of your baseball training. Be sure to visualize in a relaxing setting. Use all of your senses and emotionally feel your success. As you repeat your visualization scenes, see them with greater and greater detail.

3. Visualization sessions can take place after you learn or improve a swing or hitting mechanic. You also want to set aside time before practices and games to see yourself performing at your best. Finally, it is critical to engage in post-performance visualization to capitalize on that day's successes.

Sharpen Your Mental Game

1. Right now, relax and visualize your 5 best swings, pitches, and defensive plays. Work at creating more and more details. For example, with each run-through, make the scene brighter and sharper. Make sure to feel your successes. When you have finished, write down what this exercise was like for you.

2. The goal is to set aside time each day to work on
    visualization. Write down your personal visualization plan.
    When, where, and how will you use this powerful technique?

Chapter 11

The Confidence Hurdle

"Albert [Belle] honestly believes he is better than he is. He is very good and can be better. But almost no one on the planet is as good as Albert thinks he is." ~ Mike Hargrove

Whenever I talk to players about the mental game, one topic always comes to the forefront: confidence. Players want to know how to build and maintain confidence. Confidence is simply the belief that you can succeed in a particular situation. Right now, right here, I can do it!

If you struggle with a lack of confidence, you are not alone. All players, from time to time, experience self-doubt. Maybe they have had a string of bad at-bats or a very rough outing on the mound. The doubts *naturally* creep in. Self-doubt is almost like an automatic function for most players; negative things happen and confidence inevitably erodes. I say *most players*, because those with mentally tough personalities have the skills to reverse this natural tendency towards deterioration of confidence.

How do I build and maintain confidence?

There isn't just one thing that players can do to improve confidence; there are many things that players must do. Think of confidence as a puzzle constructed from a number of pieces. Putting all of these pieces together creates a confident player.

What are the pieces? Awareness of *for yourself* versus *against yourself* thoughts, feelings and actions; hard work and preparation; playing arrows-out; overcoming any fear failure; positive self-talk; silent bragging; expecting success; and using visualization. These pieces all work together to help you wholeheartedly believe in yourself, no matter what the situation.

Awareness of your thoughts, feelings, and actions

Before any changes can occur, you must be aware of what you are thinking, feeling, and doing. You must honestly evaluate whether the things you are thinking, feeling and doing are *for yourself* or *against yourself*. Taken together, do your thoughts, emotions, and actions enhance confidence or erode confidence? Constant self-awareness is required. *Make a commitment to think, feel, and do only those things that produce confidence.*

Preparation

One of the most important components to feeling confident about any upcoming task is to feel as though you are prepared. Whenever I am asked to give a presentation on the mental game, I want to make sure I know who the audience is, how much time I have, and what material I want to cover. I then put together the program and rehearse it. By being prepared, I feel more confident and I have the best chance of success. I am sure you have your own personal experiences, maybe in a classroom or on the field, where you have felt prepared and other times when you have not.

In baseball, the more you work at getting better in practice, the more confident you will feel during actual performance. If you are correcting a pitching or hitting mechanic and you have put the work in, you are more likely to feel a greater sense of confidence the next time out. If you get to the park and go through your pre-game routine you are more likely to feel prepared to play and more confident. Knowing that you are physically and mentally prepared is the foundation for building confidence.

Playing Arrows-Out

In Chapter 4, playing arrows-out versus arrows-in, I discussed the importance of exuding confidence and physically carrying yourself in a confident manner. Remember, arrows-out baseball refers to the energy coming from you instead of back towards you. You are in charge. You are in control. You are going to battle no matter what. You are resilient. You are tough!

In addition to changes in thoughts and emotions, arrows-out players change their physical posture and presence. There is an important mind-body relationship when it comes to confidence. I would describe it as an interaction. It is easy to quickly tell which players are feeling confident and which are not. *Even if you have some self-doubt, it is very important to physically carry yourself in a confident manner.*

By physically acting confident, several positive things are likely to happen. First, your opponents will see you as more of a threat and it may rattle their confidence. Second, by physically behaving confidently, you will automatically *feel* more confident. Your attitude will mimic your physical body. You will also find that you are more immune to negative self-talk and criticism from others.

I attended a great workshop presented by Dr. Tom Hanson (2008). He did a compelling demonstration regarding the interaction between the mind and body. Dr. Hanson asked group members to assume a posture indicating a lack of confidence (i.e., slumped shoulders, eyes and head down, etc.).

He then made a series of negative comments about the members playing abilities.

After a minute or two, he asked the group to look up, take a few breaths, and then assume a more physically confident posture (i.e., powerful posture, head up, eyes forward, etc.). For the next minute or two, Dr. Hanson proceeded to make similar negative comments about the players' abilities.

There was a noticeable difference in how the players felt and reacted. During the first phase, the players who assumed the posture reflecting a lack of confidence posture seemed to allow the negative comments to soak in. Their shoulders sunk even further; their energy level became even lower. During phase two, players listened with disregard, almost defiance and some even smirked at the negative comments. These criticisms bounced off. They were not buying it. They felt more in control. A confident posture provided their defense. *So, one of the most important things you can do is to always physically carry yourself in a confident manner.*

Overcoming the Fear of Failure

Baseball is a game of failure. No one wants to fail but it happens to all players. Chapter 5 discussed the importance of not being afraid to fail. If a player is petrified of failing, that anxiety will become the focus, taking away from focusing on the task at hand. Fearful players may say to themselves things like, "Oh no! What if I fail? It will be terrible. I am not 100% sure I can do this and if I slip up, it will be disastrous." As you can see, emphasizing failure creates self-doubt and anxiety.

The key to dealing with failure is to be able to set the fear of failure aside. By being prepared and focusing on putting forth your best efforts, rather than imagining the *what ifs* of failure, players can set the fear of failure aside. Play in the present and let the results take care of themselves.

Positive Self-Talk

In Chapter 6, The Heckler in Your Head, you learned the importance of maintaining positive self-talk. Positive self-talk is not merely cheerleading, as that only gets you so far. Instead, positive self-talk focuses on realistic self-statements that help performance. For example, when you're facing a tough pitcher, instead of saying, "He is too tough. I hope I can get a bat on it," Say something like, "Sure, he is good, but I have hit pitchers who were just as fast."

While negative self-talk is natural and automatic, you must be very aware of when it is happening and vigorously challenge these unproductive thoughts. You simply cannot afford to allow a single negative thought to linger in your mind. Negative self-talk is always an enemy.

It is also important to use your personal slogan to gain an instant boost to confidence. Also, make sure to spend time silently bragging, giving yourself credit for playing well. Use your self-talk to unconsciously program the expectation of success before each game and practice. *Positive self-talk must become a habit. It is, perhaps, your greatest weapon against a lack of confidence.*

Visualization

Visualizing yourself playing well is critical to building and maintaining self-confidence. Make sure to spend time everyday replaying your past successes and seeing yourself playing well in the future. Instead of replaying mistakes, see that great hit or that super pitch over and over in your mind. You will be conditioning your unconscious to see yourself as a quality player who is capable of succeeding!

Building and maintaining confidence takes constant awareness and hard work. Rather than a single technique, confidence requires the melding of the numerous components discussed earlier in this book. Make building confidence a priority and regularly work on this part of your mental game, and the rewards will be great!

Recap

1. Confidence is the belief that you will succeed. Building and maintaining confidence is one of the most asked-about topics in the area of mental game training.

2. There are a number of key components to developing and maintaining a confident, mentally tough personality. Awareness, preparation, playing arrows-out, ridding yourself of the fear of failure, positive self-talk, silent bragging, expecting success, and the use of visualization are all important building blocks.

Sharpen Your Mental Game

1. Feeling prepared to play is an important part of having confidence. Write down what you can do better, before practice and games, to help yourself feel prepared to perform. Be specific!

2. With a partner or in a small group, do the confident/lack of confidence posture exercise by Dr. Hanson. Write down what you experienced during each condition. If you were the person giving negative statements, what did you observe in other players?

3. Write down your personal slogan and list 10 positive self-talk
   statements. Remember, silent bragging is perfectly fine!

4. Remember playing well! List several memories related to past successes. Find a quiet place, relax, and spend 5 to 10 minutes going back to those experiences and recalling how powerful and positive you felt. Whenever you experience self-doubt, use these memories to quickly bolster confidence.

Part II

Mental Toughness in Action

"Do you know what we get to do today Brooks? We get to play baseball."
~ Dennis Quaid, as Jim Morris in The Rookie (2002)

Chapter 12

Performance: The Most Important Pitch and Other Core Beliefs

"Each pitch must be seen as another opportunity to succeed."

~ Ickes

You must play in the present

The most important pitch in any baseball game is the next pitch. In their book, *Heads-Up Baseball*, Ravizza and Hanson (1998) stress the importance of playing one pitch at a time. The upcoming pitch requires complete focus. The importance of this principle cannot be overstated. Players who are emotionally or cognitively stuck on what happened last pitch, last inning or last game will perform poorly, as will players who are worrying about the outcome of this at-bat, this inning, or this game. In order to have the best chance of success, you must play in the here and now, giving *complete priority* to the next pitch.

Allowing the pitch to be the highest priority is accomplished by focusing on the **process** of getting ready to perform, rather than the outcome. Earlier, we discussed how baseball players do not have complete control over the outcome (pitchers can make a perfect pitch and the batter still gets a hit; hitters can make a perfect swing and hit a line drive at someone). The only thing players can control is their approach to the next pitch. Focus on the process and the results will take care of themselves.

Don't panic

Another part of putting mental toughness in action is preventing panic. During baseball games and the baseball season, itself, there will be ups and downs. *It is vital that you do not panic.* Panicking does not help you or your team play better. When things go poorly, reset by using your release, and get back to using your pre-pitch routine. This is the best way to avoid getting completely out of control during a game or during the season.

Expect success

Expecting success is one of the most powerful mental game skills. As you know, I take a logical approach to what players should think, and this concept is no different. Unless there is an injury, my contention is that there is no reason why today's game cannot be your best performance ever. Players sometimes fall into the trap of merely *thinking* they might succeed or *hoping* that they will succeed. Train yourself to *expect success* before every game. Today, can you play your best baseball ever? Sure, why not?

Mentally tough athletes expect success even if their last game was unsuccessful. These mentally tough players see each game as a new opportunity and they expect to play their best. This perspective must become part of your pre-game ritual. You should approach each game as if you will play the best baseball you have ever played. Consciously work at incorporating this critical belief into your mentally tough personality. *You must expect success with the deepest conviction.*

If you have done it before, you can do it again

Here, again, is another rational thought that you must make a part of your game. From a performance standpoint, barring injury, any behavior can be repeated. If you have performed at a high level before, *you can do it again*.

For example, if you are a pitcher who falls behind a hitter 3-0, you might automatically say, "Oh no, I am in trouble. This is bad! I have to throw a strike!" Instead of this type of self-talk, it is critical to remember that you have been 3-0 before and came back to get the hitter out. *If you have done it before, you can do it again*. Reminding yourself of this rational thought changes your self-talk, emotions, and behavior. It automatically creates and keeps you in an arrows-out state, which helps performance.

The same holds true for hitters: if you are down in the count 0-2, do not let negative self-talk creep in. Instead, remind yourself that you *have* been down 0-2 and ended up getting a base hit before. Consciously, make this rational reminder one of the core beliefs of your mentally tough personality. *If you have done it before, you can do it again!*

Emotional preparation

Game day is exciting! You wake up and realize that today you have an opportunity to play baseball. What a great game! What should you do on game day to prepare yourself to succeed? When you first wake up on game day, spend a few minutes thinking about the joy of playing baseball. Reflect back on your past successes and *feel* those emotions again. Appreciate your physical body and physical abilities. Think about being successful during this upcoming game. You want to start building feelings of confidence, determination, and excitement. Let these emotions slowly build as the day progresses.

Focus increases as game time performance approaches

Playing great baseball requires excellent focus. The chapter on concentration talked about the need to focus on the right thing at the right time. It is important to remember that focus cannot be turned on and off like a faucet. I am sure you have witnessed players who have tried to go from very little focus in the dugout or on deck to the batter's box, which requires a great deal of focus. Most of the time they fail.

Think of focus as being like a funnel. Early on game day, you start thinking about playing, and that focus increases when you arrive at the ballpark. Focus becomes even more intense during pre-game warm-up and *reaches its peak during the instant of performance (when you are set to pitch or hit)*.

What are some suggestions to increase focus once you reach the ballpark? It is important that you make a conscious effort to leave the outside world behind. All of your everyday struggles, concerns, and distractions are *left outside* the ballpark. Imagine symbolically packing up all of these issues in boxes and leaving them outside the stadium. Pick a spot, maybe the outer fence or the clubhouse door, and *consciously* set your outside concerns aside. Rest assured, you will have plenty of time to try and tackle these issues after the game. Once you actually enter the stadium, you are entering a brand new world. For the next several hours, you get to have fun and play baseball. Nothing else exists. Leave everything else outside of the ballpark.

During pre-game warm-ups, your focus becomes even more intense. Stretching, throwing, and getting your body ready to perform is important. It is also important to get your mind ready to perform. You must take some time alone to gather your thoughts about the upcoming game. You should spend part of your time visualizing yourself playing well. See great swings. See yourself making great pitches or great plays. Excitement, determination and confidence are key emotions. *Expect success!*

Finally, during the game itself, employ a routine that allows you to increase your focus just prior to actual instant of performance. Pitchers, spend time using positive self-talk and visualizing success. Hitters, your at-bat starts when you pick up your helmet or grab your bat out of the rack. Minimize the chatter with other players. Begin to think about the pitcher and your hitting strategy. As you move to the on deck circle, spend some time visualizing the perfect swing. Build confidence and determination by using your empowering personal slogan on deck and as you walk to the plate. Again, focus is narrowing and is at its peak during the instant of performance.

Recap

1. In order to play well during the actual game, mentally tough players must internalize several important core beliefs about performance.

2. You must always play in the present. This is a critical core belief. Play the game one pitch at a time. Past failures cannot be changed and the focus cannot be on future worries. In order to play your best baseball, you must focus on the process of being ready for the most important pitch in any game, the next one. Use a well-practiced pre-pitch routine to stay in the present and ensure complete focus on the next pitch

3. Do not panic. There will be many ups and downs during a baseball game and a baseball season. It is important to stay on an even keel. When things go wrong, reset by using releases and pre-pitch routines.

4. Cognitively, you must consciously *expect success*, not merely hope for success or just think you might succeed. You have to *expect* to play your best baseball during the upcoming game. Expect to play well!

5. Understand the principle that if you have done it before, you can do it again. Recalling this key point during crunch time quickly boosts confidence and resets the arrows-out attitude.

6. One game day, emotionally tap into feelings of excitement, confidence and determination.

7. Increase your focus as game time performance approaches. Leave off-the-field concerns outside the ballpark. During warm-ups, take time to think about playing well. Use visualization and begin to build confidence and excitement. Prior to taking the mound or going to bat, get in the habit of minimizing distractions in order to reach peak focus at the instant of performance.

Sharpen Your Mental Game

1. Write down a detailed game day routine. Describe your routine from the time you wake up until the time you are actually on the mound or in the batter's box. Make sure to think about how you will symbolically leave everyday concerns outside the baseball park. What will be your personal cue to think about nothing but baseball (i.e., getting off of the bus, walking through the gate, going through the locker room door, etc.)?

2. Write a short paragraph about expecting success before a game. What type of self-talk statements will you use? How will you feel? How will you carry yourself? Take a few minutes to visualize yourself expecting success.

3. "If you have done it before, you can do it again." Write a
   short paragraph about this core belief. You might want to
   write about a situation where you wish you could have had
   this mindset or about a situation where that thought has
   helped you in the past. Make sure to remind yourself of this
   belief during practices and games.

Chapter 13

Winning the Instant of Performance

"Let your performance do the thinking."
~ H. Jackson Brown Jr.

The ultimate goal in baseball is to win the instant of performance (IOP). Remember, the IOP is actually a very brief period of time (typically 2-5 seconds), which begins when both the pitcher and hitter are at-the-ready, and that ends when the baseball reaches home plate. Assuming that the physical talent level is approximately equal, the player *who is in the best mental state* will have the *greatest chance of success* on that particular pitch. Again, there are no guarantees of success, as we have already discussed that outcome is not completely within our control. But, being in the optimal state of mind in terms of what you are feeling, thinking, and doing gives you the best chance.

Just what is the optimal state of mind? In order to answer this question, we must look at what researchers tell us about being in the zone. Now, I am sure you are familiar with the zone. The zone is that magical physical and mental state when everything falls into place. You are *feeling* it.

There are numerous books and articles that discuss the characteristics of zone states; Sugarman gives an excellent description in *Winning the Mental Way* (1999). She describes players who are in zone states as feeling confident, completely focused, relaxed, and in control. These same players characterize playing baseball as being fun, effortless, and automatic. Do you experience these things when you are in the zone?

My contention is that by using a quality pre-pitch routine, you can train yourself to mimic the characteristics of being in the zone. By mimicking the zone, true zone states may occur more frequently and last longer. Mimicking the zone allows you to play at the highest level possible, automatically. In a sense, players become well-oiled, efficient pitching, hitting, and fielding machines.

In order to mimic the zone, players must be feeling, thinking, and doing specific things.

Feeling: In order to achieve the best chance of success, players need to experience the right emotions with the appropriate intensity. As we have discussed in earlier chapters, excess anxiety and anger hurt performance while confidence and determination are beneficial. The goal, then, is to foster the positive emotions and control the negative ones by monitoring and changing self-talk, using deep breathing exercises, and by using releases.

Thinking: During the instant of performance you want zero conscious thoughts. Plan your strategy before you get in the batter's box or before you start your pitching motion. This is the time for any positive self-talk. Once you are ready to perform, all conscious thinking should cease.

Doing: At the instant of performance you will be relying completely on muscle memory. One of my favorite things to tell players is, "You know how to hit. You have taken tens of thousands of swings. Get your mind out of the way and let your body do what it is supposed to do."

Pre-Pitch Routines: More Than Just Fixing Your Gloves and Tapping the Plate

The ideal pre-pitch hitting routine should look something like this:

1. Based on the count, the game situation, and signs from the coach you will have a plan before each pitch. *Have your plan, and commit to it **before** you get into the box.* For example, if the count is 2-0 and your plan is to look for a fastball, do not re-think it once you are in the box. If you feel the need to change your plan for any reason, call time and step out.

2. Once you get your plan, *step confidently into the box with your back foot.* Take charge of the batter's box. You are the boss and you set the pace. Hank Aaron said, "I never smile when I have a bat in my hands. That's when you've got to be serious. When I get out on the field, nothing's a joke to me. I don't feel like I should walk around with a smile on my face." He also said, "The pitcher has got only a ball. I've got a bat." (Rubin, 2004). Now, that is the arrows-out attitude you want to take each time you step in the batter's box!

3. Once your foot is in the box, take a nice slow, deep (abdominal) breath. Make sure your core (the chest and stomach) is relaxed. If you still feel tension, take another deep breath.

4. As you take your breath, have a last conscious thought. This should be your personal slogan. Powerful and confidence building, it is a signal that you are ready to do some damage with your bat.

5. Next, look closely at your focal point. Remember, this focal point is usually the same spot on your bat, but can be a spot on home plate, your shoe, or even something out in the

distance. *The key is to always have the same focal point.*
Study the details, allowing all conscious thinking to stop. Do
not try to push thoughts away but let your thoughts quickly
fade or drift away. With practice, you will get very skilled at
turning your conscious thinking off.

6. From the focal point move your eyes ***directly*** out to the
   pitcher's release point. If this seems uncomfortable, you can
   glance at a spot on the plate, or the ground, before moving
   your eyes out to the release point. The key is to look
   somewhere where there are no distractions. If your
   concentration is ever broken while you are in the box, call
   time out and start your routine over.

7. With the core relaxed and all noises, thoughts, and
   distractions cleared, *you experience 100% narrow external
   focus.* You have laser-like focus on the baseball coming out of
   the release point. This is the optimal state. This is
   mimicking the zone.

8. The last step is to completely trust your body. No thinking;
   just react to the ball. This means that you must trust your
   go/no go decision and swing completely. Have confidence that
   your body knows how to hit. During the actual instant of
   performance, there is no need to coach yourself, focus on body
   position, or do any type of conscious analysis. You are an
   efficient hitting machine. Trust yourself!

9. The pre-pitch routine is the same for every single pitch. No
   matter what the game situation, the routine stays the same.
   When negative things happen, like a bad swing or a bad call,
   simply go back to your routine and reset. A well-practiced,
   quality routine gives you the best chance of success.

Recap

1. The instant of performance is the brief period that begins when the pitcher and hitter are at-the-ready and ends when the baseball crosses home plate. The primary goal for both the pitcher and hitter is to win the instant of performance. If the talent level is equal, whichever player is in the best mental state has the greatest chance of a positive outcome.

2. The optimal mental state is patterned after what players feel, think, and do when they are in the zone. Your goal is to use a quality pre-pitch routine to mimic the characteristics of the zone before each and every pitch.

3. The pre-pitch routine includes such things as: approaching the plate in a confident manner, getting your plan, taking a slow, deep breath, using your focal point to clear all thoughts, completely trusting your body.

4. The pre-pitch routine is practiced until it becomes an automatic part of your game. It is performed before each and every pitch, regardless of the score or situation. A quality, well-practiced pre-pitch routine gives you the best chance of success.

Sharpen Your Mental Game

1. Write a detailed description of your pre-pitch routine. Be sure to include all of the steps to help you relax, clear your mind, improve focus, and to trust your body. Spend a minimum of 5-10 minutes a day practicing your pre-pitch routine.

2. Spend time throughout each day working on the individual components of your routine. For example, practice taking a series of deep breaths and relaxing while you are walking around. Practice studying your focal point; letting conscious thoughts go; and immediately shifting to a distant object. Write down your experiences regarding these practice sessions.

3. This drill is designed to give you the feel of playing
    without any conscious thought. During batting practice,
    go through your routine, really paying attention to getting
    relaxed and clearing you mind. Try to get to zero
    thoughts before the ball is pitched. You are just focusing
    on the process of getting ready. Do not worry about the
    outcome of your swing. This *process only* drill should be
    done on a regular basis. Incorporate this drill into your
    regular batting practices by treating the last few swings
    of each round as if it is a game situation. Write down
    your experiences with this drill.

4. Practice a similar pre-performance routine when playing other sports, musical instruments, or video games. Use your deep breathing to relax before performance, use a focal point to clear your mind, and completely trust your body. What did you notice about your performance?

Chapter 14

Heard in the Dugout: Player Comments

"Remember, you do not have to play baseball,
you get to play baseball." ~ Brian Cain

I am always interested in how players that I have worked with view the mental game.   I often use anonymous surveys to gain insight into what they think about my training program.   I thought I would give you a glimpse of what these players are saying about the mental game and the impact it has on performance.   Below, you will find a few sample questions and player responses.   I hope by reading their comments, you will be inspired to take your game to the next level!

How do you build and maintain your confidence?

"I have a very simple way of building and maintaining my confidence. Whether I am in the batter's box or not I know I can hit whatever pitcher is on the mound.   In my head I have already told myself that the pitcher does not stand a chance when I'm hitting."

"I stay confident by visualizing success during down time. It helps me remember that I have done it before so I will be able to do it again."

"I tell myself that I am the best player on the field. I put hard work day in and day out to achieve my personal goals. If you know you have worked hard and have performed well in the past, it is okay to be confident but not cocky."

"Playing arrows out and visualizing success, not failure, helps me the most. You use the good images in your head, therefore, you are confident."

"My confidence comes from trusting in my abilities. I know I am a good player or else I would not be here. I can do whatever my team needs me to do at any given moment."

"I build and maintain confidence through self talk and visualization. Coming off of injuries and setbacks, it is critical to maintain the same confidence and always keep those thoughts in your mind bank."

"Positive imagery allows you to replay past successes. This basically tricks your mind and body into thinking you have already succeeded in that performance. It also works with thinking about success before your at-bat, game, season, etc. You can develop that confidence every day, no matter the weather or facility availability. It is a vital aspect of baseball at any level."

"Building confidence can be done through the mental game and through practice. Players need to always practice playing arrows out and not feel sorry for themselves."

"Visualize, visualize, visualize. This is almost as good as really hitting the ball. You can take 100 swings and not even get out of bed."

How important is using a pre-pitch routine?

"It is extremely important. It allows you to reduce anxiety and it also allows you to stay in the zone. By developing a routine, you can have confidence that you are ready to hit, regardless of your past performances."

"As a high school player I had no idea that there was any such thing as a pre-pitch routine. I just did whatever. Now in college it has tremendously changed the way I pitch. The routine makes me more confident, helps me stay under control, and helps me release when things are not going my way."

"The pre-pitch routine gets me back in the zone. I leave all distractions aside and get back into the game with my routine. Deep breathing allows me to focus in on the game and not worry what is going on around or behind me."

"I see it as like a security blanket. The situation and score will change with every at bat, but I will always have the same routine to help bring me confidence. The routine makes it seem like I've been there before. It helps me relieve pressure and doubt."

What has been the most important thing you have learned about the mental game?

"The most important thing for me is to be confident before I step into the batter's box. Nothing gets the pitcher more nervous than seeing nine confident guys stepping up to the plate, ready to crush him."

"Visualization is the key to understanding the mental game. Visualization tricks your body into doing more work than you have had to do, which results in more success."

"The focal point is the most important thing. It helps me to relax and gather myself when things are not going my way. It's an escape for me to forget the bad and focus on the good."

"Doing a quality pre-pitch routine has helped me focus on each pitch individually. My routine allows me to concentrate fully on each pitch. This has made me both a clutch and a more relaxed hitter."

"Hands down the most important thing for me has been the relaxation training. The deep breath before every pitch really works. It actually breaks the at-bat into single pitches, instead of that at-bat feeling like a cumulative ordeal."

"The most important thing I have learned is how to use a release and not let things out of my control affect the next play or pitch which I can control."

"Becoming aware of my thoughts when I'm playing has really helped. Negative thoughts tend to creep into your mind and without monitoring and changing those thoughts; it can be detrimental to my performance."

"Learning to create the zone in situations where there is little or no pressure makes doing it in a big game a lot easier. Routines are everything."

"The best thing for me was learning how to deal with failure and let it go. Think about the next pitch. Also, learning how to block out all thoughts other than 'crush the ball' has been a great help."

"The most important thing I learned was how to take deep breathes and focus on something small or distant. Whenever things start to go bad, I walk away from the mound and focus on the tree tops and escape for a split second. That helps me regroup so things don't start to snowball into a worse situation."

"The most important thing was to believe in myself and not beat myself up when I made an error."

"The most important skill I learned was to believe that I am capable of controlling my reaction to failure."

What advice would you give a player just learning about the mental game?

"Treat it like any other aspect of the game—hitting, pitching, throwing, running. The mental game is actually more important, but no one tells you so until you start playing at the higher levels, like college."

"The most important thing is to be positive. You can't get anywhere with a negative attitude."

"The mental game is vital to your success on the field. Playing arrows out and using visualization really helps."

"Repetition is the key. When visualizing hitting, I had to visualize off the field in order for me to build it into my head. I needed to make my brain react automatically, so when I was in a clutch situation, I was firing on all cylinders."

"My advice would be to stay positive no matter how you are playing. It is a long season and failure is going to be part of it. Stay positive and don't let it affect your game."

"Work on visualizing your successes instead of focusing on failures. Some players probably think that they should learn from their mistakes. I believe you can learn as much from your successes."

"Spend the time to develop a great pre-pitch routine. Do your routine every time, before each pitch and stick to it. Do not change anything. Make sure you take your deep breaths!"

"The mental game is something that most players overlook and feel is not that important. My best advice is to keep an open mind about the techniques and aspects that surround the mental game. The mental game needs to be practiced over and over again just like the physical side of the game."

"Going 0-7 in a two game stretch is not bad. I have done it plenty this year. The key is to get back to your mental game basics, like the routine, so it doesn't turn into an 0-15 or 0-20 slump. Mental training has helped me become a more consistent hitter."

"Try to play highlight reels in your mind before competing. See yourself having success and then you go out and do it."

"Learn how to cope with failure so you can maintain consistency at the plate."

"The key to consistency is a deliberate dose of imagined success prior to and immediately following games. The best advice I was ever given was to replay my best games in my head before each and every game."

"Give it time. Don't think that you are going to master the mental game in a few days. Go through the routine over and over, so it becomes second nature. It takes time to master the mental game."

Chapter 15

Troubleshooting the Mental Game

"All things are difficult before they become easy."
~ Thomas Fuller

Having worked with hundreds of players, I have found there are some common pitfalls regarding achieving and maintaining a great mental game. Here are some common concerns, along with some possible solutions.

Pseudo-slumps

This is a term that I use to explain a situation when a player *thinks* he is in a slump, when in reality he is not. This typically occurs when a player has a stretch of hitless games. Automatically, he assumes something is terribly wrong with his swing and this causes him to panic. The self-talk goes something like this, "Oh no, I can't hit anymore! This is terrible! What am I doing wrong? Is it my stance? What about my hands? Man, I am in a horrible slump...how am I going to get out of it? I need to fix my swing right now!"

In reality, his swing is fine. He is just hitting into some bad luck. In baseball you sometimes can do everything mentally and mechanically right and not get a hit. Because the player is so focused on statistics, he fails to see that he is having quality at-bats. The *real* danger, here, is that the panicked player makes adjustments to an already good swing! This, in turn, creates a real slump.

To avoid pseudo-slumps, you must avoid panicking. Do not jump to the conclusion that something is terribly wrong based on the box score. (I once had a player tell me he was in a slump after going 0-8 in the season-opening doubleheader. He hit the ball hard 7 out of 8 times). How do you avoid falling into this trap? Carefully and objectively evaluate your at-bats. Focus on the process of hitting, rather than statistics. How many quality at-bats did you have? How did you feel at the plate? If you are having quality at-bats, *keep doing exactly what you are doing*. The hits will start to fall. Baseball has a great way of evening things out!

Failing to keep track of what you are doing right

Too often, players and coaches can fall into the trap of being problem-oriented. One of the most important things you can do is to notice when you are doing things well. One player I worked with kept track of exactly what he was thinking, feeling and doing when things were going well. He kept track of how he prepared for each at-bat from being in the hole, to on-deck, to his approach at the plate. He wrote down how he handled failure when it occurred and gave himself a pat on the back for his good efforts. I would suggest you do the same. Remember to also spend some time (just 5 to 10 minutes a day) using visualization to replay successes. See it, feel it, and believe it!

Moping about playing time

Every athlete wants to be a starter and play all the time. Baseball players are no different. However, you may find yourself in a position where you are not starting, maybe not even getting into the game. Is it disappointing? Yes. Frustrating?

Yes. It is critical, however, that you cope with these emotions effectively.

It is not uncommon to see players moping, complaining, and, unfortunately, creating dissention on a team because they are not playing as much as they want to. Mentally tough players do not respond this way. They focus on what they can control and let go of what they cannot control. Players do not fill out the lineup card, but players can control how hard they work in practice to get better. As a player, it is your responsibility to control any negative attitude towards teammates, coaches, and the game itself. I personally have never seen a situation where a disgruntled player has helped himself play better or helped his team win. Focus on getting better every day so that when the opportunities arise, you will make the most of them.

Being unable to get to zero thoughts during the instant of performance

One of the key goals is to reduce conscious thinking during the instant of performance. Remember, you will use a solid, well-practiced routine to accomplish a thought-free state. Most players learn this pre-pitch routine quickly. It is very effective in stopping conscious thoughts.

However, some players have a very difficult time getting to zero thoughts. For these players, I suggest they modify their routine to incorporate one single, last thought. The players will still do their thinking outside of the box or off the rubber. They will still take their deep breaths and use a focal point. However, right after the focal point, the player will make a simple self-statement, as his eyes move towards the target area. I have had players tell me that they say things like, "It is ripping time!" or "Nobody better!" Sometimes, it can be a single word like "seams." The key is to use the same phrase or word every time, regardless of the game situation.

Another solution to not being able to get to zero thoughts is to briefly hum a song. Again, like the last phrase or word, it must be the same song, no matter what the situation.

Thinking too much and trying too hard

One of the most common things I hear from players is that they do not have a quiet mind. They are thinking too much. They feel tension because they are trying too hard. It has been said many times before, baseball isn't always about *making* things happen; it is about *letting* things happen.

The solution to thinking too much and trying too hard is to get back to basics: doing a quality pre-pitch routine. Your routine is your best friend. It is your support. The routine helps you play in the present, controls anxiety and anger, and improves concentration and focus. Focus on the process of your pre-pitch routine, rather than being fixated on the impossible task of trying to completely control the outcome.

Failing to work on the mental game throughout the entire season

Often players will be very enthusiastic about working on their mental game during the pre-season but will seem to forget about it once the season begins. It is critical to not give up on the mental game once the season starts. You must continue to be aware of what you are thinking, feeling and doing. Practice positive self-talk, expect success, and use visualization throughout the year.

References

Amberry, T. (n.d.). *Make every free throw*. Retrieved from

http://www.freethrow.com/

Amberry, T., & Reed, P. (1996). *Free throw: 7 steps to success at the free throw line*. New York, NY: Harper Paperbacks.

Balwin, D. (2009, September 17). Unraveling the batter's brain. *Baseball Analysts*, Retrieved from http://baseballanalysts.com/archives/2009/09/ unraveling_the.php

Carlstedt, R. (2004). *Critical moments during competition: A mind-body model of sport performance when it counts most*. New York, NY: Psychology Press.

Doidge, N. (2007). *The brain that changes itself*. New York, NY: Viking Press.

Ellis, A., & Harper, R. (1975). *A new guide to rational living*. New York, NY: Prentice- Hall.

Gordon, D. (2008). *Your brain on Cubs: Inside the heads of players and fans*. New York, NY: Dana Press.

Hanson, T. (2008, January). Learn how to play with confidence, focus, and mental toughness [Workshop]. Clearwater, FL.

Hanson, T. (2008). *Jeter's secret to confidence.* Retrieved from http://www.baseballconfidence.com/

Isaac, A. (1992). Mental practice- does it work in the field? *The Sport Psychologist, 6,* 192-198.

Iverson practice! (2006). [Web]. Retrieved from http://www.youtube.com/watch?v=eGDBR2L5kzI

John, T., & Valenti, D. (1991). *TJ: My 26 years in baseball.* New York, NY: Bantum Books.

Libet, B. (1985). Unconscious cerebral initiative and the role of conscious will in voluntary action. *Behavioral and Brain Sciences, 8,* 529-566.

Libet, B, Gleason, C.A., Wright, E.W., & Pearl, D.K. (1983). Time of conscious intention to act in relation to onset of cerebral activity (readiness-potential): The unconscious initiation of a freely voluntary act. *Brain, 106,* 623-642.

Newman, M. & Berkowitz, B. (1986). *How to be your own best friend.* New York, NY: Ballantine Books.

Nideffer, R. M. (1993). Concentration and attention control training. In J.M. Williams (Ed.), *Applied sport psychology: Personal growth to peak performance.* Mountain View, CA: Mayfield.

Olney, B. (2004, June 24). The confidence man. *New York Magazine*, Retrieved from http://nymag.com/nymetro/news/sports/features/9375/

Pedro Alvarez home run vs. Memphis - 2008 Vanderbilt. (2008). [Web]. Retrieved from http://www.youtube.com/watch?v=zlhTPNr

Ravizza, K. & Hanson, T. (1998). *Heads-up baseball : Playing the game one pitch at a time.* New York, NY: McGraw-Hill.

Ringer, R. (1977). *Looking out for #1.* New York, NY: Fawcett.

Rubin, L. (2004). *The quotable baseball fanatic.* New York, NY: The Lyons Press.

Sugarman, K. (1999). *Winning the mental way: A practical guide to team building and mental training.* New York, NY: Step-Up Publications.

Schwartz, A. (2008). No experience needed for a

Tampa Bay rookie. *The New York Times*, Retrieved

from http://www.nytimes.com/2008/10/21/sports/

baseball/21rays.html

Short, S, & Monsma, E. (2006). Onwards with the

evolution of imagery research in sport psychology.

Athletic Insight, *8*(3), Retrieved from

http://www.athleticinsight.com/Vol8Iss3

/ImageryResearch.htm

Wolpe, J. (1958). *Psychotherapy by reciprocal inhibition.*

Stanford, CA: Stanford University Press.

Yue, G, & Cole, K.J. (1992). Strength increases from the

motor program: Comparison of training with maximal

voluntary and imagined muscle contractions. *Journal of*

Neurophysiology, *67*(5), 1114-1123.

61046615R00089

Made in the USA
Charleston, SC
12 September 2016